Medi

A Buddhist View

Jinananda
(Duncan Steen)

ⓦindhorse Publications

Published by
Windhorse Publications
169 Mill Road
Cambridge
CB1 3AN
United Kingdom

info@windhorsepublications.com
www.windhorsepublications.com

First Edition 2000
Second Edition 2012

Typeset and designed by Ben Cracknell Studios
Cover design by Deborah Harward and Marlene Eltschig
Cover image © Borut Trdina
Printed by Bell & Bain Ltd, Glasgow

British Library Cataloguing in Publication Data:
A catalogue record for this book is available from the British Library

ISBN: 9781 907314 06 3

Dedication

To my son, Antoine, with love.

About the Author

Jinananda, also known as Duncan Steen, was born in Bedford, England, in 1952 and became a member of the Western Buddhist Order (now the Triratna Buddhist Order) in 1986. His name means 'Bliss of the Conqueror'. He is also the author of *Warrior of Peace* (Windhorse Publications), *The Middle Way: the story of Buddhism, and Karma and Rebirth* (Naxos AudioBooks), and has edited for publication the lectures and a number of seminars of his teacher Sangharakshita. He teaches meditation and mindfulness at London's City Lit, and meditation and Buddhism at the West London Buddhist Centre.

Acknowledgements

I would like to thank my meditation teachers, Kamalashila and Vajradaka, and my tireless editor, Vidyadevi, who gave my ramblings the lineaments of a book. Thanks also to those who gave encouragement and support and invaluable advice and criticism: Jan Parker, Nagabodhi, Kulananda, Claudia Campos, Kamalashila, and Vessantara, and to Dharmashura, Shantavira, Jnanasiddhi, and Padmavajri for persisting in the struggle to get a book out of me. And thanks to Jinamitra as always. For this revised edition I must thank Jnanasiddhi, and Jinamitra again, and Priyananda, for his always courteous chivvying.

Contents

Preface

I wrote the bulk of this book ten years ago and I am glad to be able to look at it again. This is partly because I have slightly changed the way I teach meditation over that time. But I also welcome the qualification 'a Buddhist view'. I don't want to insert Buddhism in a clunky way, but rather to open up the goal and scope of the practice of meditation, to make it a radical, transformative, waking-up practice rather than a safe, patching-up, therapeutic tool.

You don't of course have to be a Buddhist to take up meditation and other Buddhist practices like mindfulness. But I think it helps. It is true that these practices can be employed as techniques to sort things out for you at some level without taking on the whole Buddhist package. However, the reason these practices work so well is that they come out of the Buddha's direct experience of how things really are. Buddhist teaching is designed to challenge our unconsidered assumptions at the deepest level, to keep us looking and listening for what is really going on. And without that challenge, our meditation practice will keep running up against the limits of what we are prepared to experience.

According to Buddhism our suffering arises out of skewed views about how things are. Meditation and mindfulness practices, if done properly, actually change the way we experience things; that is, they change our views. Clearly this result can be pushed forward quite substantially if we can be more aware of what the tradition has found to be unhelpful views, and what it has found to be helpful ones. I look at the whole subject of views later on in the book, and I bring them up in other contexts as they arise. But to begin with we'll look at three fundamental ways of looking at things that support Buddhist practice.

The first of these ways of looking is *conditionality*. What this means is that nothing has a stand-alone existence; everything comes into being because of conditions. From this emerges a significant initial definition of what you are doing in meditation: you are setting up conditions for an ever more positive mental state to arise. Conditions include: where you practise, and with whom; your shrine, perhaps; your posture; and of course the particular practice you do. But it's easy to forget the raft of conditions you bring to the practice from the way you lead your life and have lived your life. In a sense the most positive mental state is one that is fully open to the natural results of all these conditions. Without understanding this guiding principle of conditionality there is almost inevitably a tendency to try to force results, to try to grab something unearned.

So an important shift in attitude that meditation requires is that, whatever your experience of yourself at this moment may be, you can work with it more effectively by acknowledging that you have earned it at some level.

This brings us to the second principle I want to mention, which is *responsibility*. To practise meditation effectively you need to take responsibility for your suffering. For all of it. It should be said very clearly that this is not about being judgemental towards yourself or relieving others of their responsibility. It is a practical stratagem for working more effectively with your mental states.

For a Buddhist, being a victim – the blaming innocent – is not a healthy position. Nor is it useful to dump blame on yourself, to play the miserable sinner. But it is possible to say, 'I knew what I was doing – I played my part in this somewhere along the line, and I will take the consequences': you are reclaiming your freedom, you are taking charge of your life. Sometimes you may be dealt a very difficult hand. Sometimes things happen that you can't do much about. But you can at least choose how you respond to your experience. This is not about blaming people in general for their misfortunes, thinking that they somehow 'deserve' them. It is a personal practice of taking responsibility for your own experience. Sometimes it seems like our experience doesn't or shouldn't belong to us, but taking ownership of it frees up emotional energy to work more creatively with it.

So in meditation you take responsibility for whatever state of mind you are in: you laid the conditions for this state of mind to establish its hold. Being responsible means understanding that you created this; it also, crucially, means that you can create something different in the future. You are not stuck. You can start, moment by moment, to change those conditions. People often talk about the need for 'acceptance'. This is not really a Buddhist position. Instead of talking about 'acceptance', a Buddhist will work towards taking responsibility for their mental state. You take, in a sense, what's coming to you.

The third principle is *paying attention*. I am told that scientists have performed tests to prove that meditation works, that it has a positive physical effect on the brain. Apparently it 'rewires' the prefrontal cortex. This is clearly very interesting research. However, it is a rather non-Buddhist way of testing meditation practices. The Buddha once advised some rather sceptical villagers (in the *Kālāma Sutta*) that they should not accept teachings simply because those teachings have been given the thumbs up by some higher authority. He said, check them out for yourself. Today, that higher authority is not religious, but scientific. The danger of lapping up scientific approbation is that you are thereby submitting the Buddhist perspective to a higher authority. The

Buddha's advice was to put the pronouncements of people claiming to be experts (including of course Buddhists) to the test of your own experience.

So I always say to my students, 'I'm going to tell you how you should go about this practice, how to sit, how to work with your mind, but to do it properly you need to submit everything I say to the evidence of your own experience. If it works, fine; if it doesn't work, try it a different way. Experiment.'

Buddhist meditation is a practice of being true to your experience. This may sound like a fine idea, but there is a good reason why it tends to remain an idea, and why therefore we tend to avoid meditation. Being true to your experience means getting behind the idea of what is going on, behind the label, the interpretation, to the inchoate, ungraspable, unfathomable experience of this moment. In meditation we slow down the current of thoughts that tells us a familiar story of what is going on in order to experience something much more mysterious and difficult.

Something I often notice when I am teaching is that people want to know what is supposed to be happening, what they are supposed to experience, to feel. Now it is true that there are certain things that people who meditate may sometimes experience – and we shall be looking at these – but the way towards these states of mind is to be prepared to sit with what is actually going on, however uncomfortable, confusing, and messy that may be.

The method actor Robert de Niro observes of his approach to acting, 'People don't try to show their feelings, they try to hide them.' That is, his truth as an actor is in revealing an attempt not to reveal something. If he is right, our complaints of being misunderstood are a bit of a smokescreen. We are afraid of our cover being blown, of being found out, of not being who we are supposed to be. Which in a way is okay. Except that the conspiracy goes all the way to the top – we inevitably buy into our self-image. We buy into a grand myth of being real: karaoke bars the world over echo to the words 'I did it my way.' It is a comforting delusion. A saying by a Jewish mystic called Zushya of Hanipol offers an alternative path; he says, 'When I get to heaven, they won't ask me, "Zushya, why weren't you Moses?" They will ask me, "Zushya, why weren't you Zushya?"' The question isn't rhetorical. It is not a reproach, I think. It wants an answer: what is getting in the way? We can't jump straight into being true to ourselves. First we must sit with something rather messier. All the stuff that stops us being ourselves.

Even when people try to express the truth of their feelings, they may best do this by not being able to do so. Eloquence is convincing, but there is a deeper truth in incoherence, in language breaking down. The deepest truth of us is always unutterable. And yet instinctively we refer our experience to our thinking for its validation. We trust our thinking to tell us the truth of what is going on. And this is where we manufacture our suffering. It is also where it can be relieved. In meditation we work with the fact that the mind produces suffering.

We assume that our thinking is the seat of our being. But the expression 'lost in thought' actually expresses what is really going on. Our thoughts are not where our home is. By living in our thoughts we are exiles. Where our real home might be is tricky to say. In a way that is the point. Some people say it is the body, but I think the body is more a channel that leads us home. Ultimate reality is our home. It is here and now, and it is not a special piece of what is happening. We imagine that we are on a journey, that life is a journey, but we were at home from the beginning. This is not an easy thing to accept.

Most people who take up meditation expect it to fix their lives in some way, to make their lives more comfortable and relaxed. Now I'm not sure that this has quite been my experience. If anything, I suspect it has enabled me to take on more stress, to be in a sense more relaxed about experiencing tension and unpleasantness. It all becomes in a sense less of a problem. And I think this is nearer to the real purpose of meditation. I think the modern tendency is to be less and less tolerant of any kind of difficulty or insecurity. We are encouraged by a certain credit-card company, for example, to 'take the waiting out of wanting'. Yes, meditation does make life easier to handle, less of a problem, but it is also about being able to tolerate the ultimate stress and insecurity of facing the nature of reality.

So another expectation that needs to be nuanced a little is the idea that meditation is going to bring a deeper meaning to life. What I've noticed about an experience of terrible loss of some kind is that you also lose a sense of meaning. You feel alienated from everyone else going about their ordinary lives. You look at your pre-catastrophe life and you can make no connection with where you are now. This is because one's sense of meaning was never connected to the nature of reality, to how things really are. So again, my own experience is that meditation in its deeper processes tends to dismantle one's sense of meaning where it is based on unreal views.

Ultimately meditation should challenge our unconsidered values and sense of meaning to allow something very different to come through. My aim in this book is to clarify the practice of meditation, but to do so in a way that makes it an exercise in not knowing, a sense that our understanding is rooted in darkness, that it draws its nourishment from where it must be in the dark. This nourishment, the meaning of things, lies all around us.

There is a line by the Australian poet Les Murray: 'Everything except language knows the meaning of existence.' I was reminded of this line on holiday in Venezuela when we had a few days in the rainforest. Our guide had learnt English, but he still belonged to the forest. And as I watched him move so easily through his world, I asked him why he didn't wear shoes. I'm not sure if it was simply that he had not learnt to say 'I know this world', as we would. But what he said was, 'The forest knows me.' I think meditation is an exercise in rediscovering this basic trust, this faith in the reality of things and making our home there.

1

Introduction

Wonders are many, but none more
Wondrous and unfathomed than Man,
The wanderer, who strides the rage
Of winter winds over grey seas.

Sophocles, *Antigone*

A curious assumption lies behind our pursuit of happiness. We assume that in order to find life deeply satisfying we have to find things – movies, relationships, food, drink, holidays, sex, books, meditation – that will deliver this deep satisfaction. The conclusion we draw from this is that the more gratifying experiences we can fit into as short a time as possible, the happier we will be. Indeed, we are prepared to go to a lot of trouble – even a lot of misery – to get our hands on as many of life's satisfying goods as we can.

But if we look a little more closely at our pleasures, they consist in those activities – whether we call them work or play – to which we offer no resistance. Someone who is fully absorbed in watching a film, changing a nappy, or climbing a mountain is happy because she experiences no conflict. She doesn't feel boredom, resentment, shame, anxiety, greed. Her mind isn't somewhere else.

Meditation is the practical application of this simple idea: that satisfaction, happiness, absorption, are not the end-product of some gratifying thing or experience, but a way of going about things. Happiness is something we bring to life, not something life delivers to us. This may sound like a nice idea, but it is a profoundly strange one. It suggests that we can develop the state of absorption we call happiness independently of whether or not we find ourselves in happy circumstances. And this is where meditation comes in.

The experience of feeling disconnected from things, from other people, from a deeper appreciation of the world around us, is really the experience of a disconnected self. The faster our minds flick from one channel of our experience to another, looking for something sufficiently gripping to hold our attention, the more fragmentary and superficial that experience tends to be.

This vampiric searching for nourishment from the life around us is essentially unconscious. In *Dracula*, the sinister count is recognized as a vampire by the fact that he has no reflection in a mirror; his nature is that he never sees himself. He is also immortal – he has refused the gift of impermanence – but his fear of loss, of disconnection, actually disconnects him from life and light. And only two things will reduce him to a handful of dust: exposing him to daylight or driving a stake through his heart. To put it less drastically, the life drained of meaning that Dracula symbolizes is vulnerable to the light of awareness, and to the opening of the heart. And the two basic practices of Buddhist meditation I shall be introducing in this book are concerned with cultivating these qualities of awareness and open-heartedness.

Both are straightforward exercises for ordinary life. However, I have raised the image of Count Dracula in his life-or-death struggle with his old adversary, Dr Van Helsing, in order to emphasize that meditation represents something quite uncompromising, a radical change of direction for the psyche. At the same time, this profound change of direction involves a patient acceptance, an openness, a great tenderness towards our own states of mind as they start to reveal themselves to us in meditation. In traditional Buddhist terms, wisdom comes with an equally uncompromising compassion, which excludes no one, not even ourselves.

There is no one experiencing our mental states from the outside. We are them. If we want to experience different states, we have to become them. And that process begins the moment we form an intention to meditate. Meditation is a practice, not a performance. You can start whenever you can clear a short space in your day. Now, for example. To try it out, all you have to do is put aside for a few moments all the things you have to worry about today and sit down: still, relaxed, softly awake, eyes gently closed. Then begin to appreciate these empty moments in themselves. These moments are owed to no one. Nor are they an investment for some future pay-off. You don't even have to make the most of them. Savour them at your ease. Just watch them bubble out of your mind . . . then notice the baggage of reactions with which you want to weigh them down. . . Now see if you can be patient enough to release the bright, steady, spacious quality that is present in those moments.

Part One

Stillness

2

Stepping Out
of the World

*In every consulting room, there ought to be two rather
frightened people: the patient and the psychoanalyst. If they
are not, one wonders why they are bothering to find out what
everyone knows.*

W.R. Bion

Why meditate? To let go of stress? To become more focused? To
fathom the mysteries of the universe? Whatever your purpose
may be – and it will probably change over time – you won't be able
to meditate without it. Meditation does not appear to be a very
useful activity viewed from one's 'got a busy day' perspective, so
we are going to have to find ways to shape our intention into a
purpose that our everyday mind can readily appreciate. Whatever
name we give our purpose – calming down, for example, or
becoming more focused, even exploring the mysteries of human
consciousness – it is a good idea to keep it in mind. The easiest way
to do this is to attend a regular meditation group. The quotation
from Sophocles at the beginning of the introduction is intended
to be a bit of a warning that finding peace of mind can be a long

and occasionally difficult haul, and it is only fair to say that most people who try to meditate without regular contact with others on the same journey will drift back to port.

What may start off as a bit of a struggle to fit meditation into your everyday life can become an understanding, even a rapport, between the two areas of experience. You can be sure that your meditation is beginning to take off when you become aware that it is having an effect on the rest of your life. But you will also gradually become aware that your everyday life – particularly the way you treat other people, as well as the way you treat yourself – is having an effect on your meditation. It should begin to become clear, then, that ethics is no less a training of the mind than is meditation. That is to say, our actions are not just things we do; at the same time as they express our being, they also change it.

The fundamental Buddhist insight is that nothing happens in isolation. So there is a connection between meditation and whatever else you do. But even though the aim is to stay centred, aware, and kind in the storms and doldrums of everyday activity, anyone who meditates will need to find a way to navigate the transition. Try to establish a non-negotiable time to meditate. That will help you, and everyone else who is part of your life, to support your intention. If you have been rushing around, you will need to step down a few gears before you meditate, perhaps by engaging in some quiet, simple, unhurried activity: sweeping the floor, say, or watering the garden, or having a cup of tea, or doing a few yoga stretches.

Now you are ready to start. So, where would be a good place? If you are going to close your eyes it won't matter where you sit, right? Well, let's think about it. When you sit down to meditate for the first time, it is natural to feel a little apprehensive. This is a good thing. It means you are open to the possibility that something new is going to happen. If you feel 'at home' with meditation, if you have settled down with something safe and familiar, you are not going to be so open to this possibility. To maintain something of the wide-eyed freshness that the Zen tradition calls 'beginner's mind', we need to nourish this slight sense of apprehensiveness.

Our knowledge has banished our fear of the old gods, but in meditation we need to reconnect with a sense of moving through a world we don't understand. We are entering a different realm in which different rules apply; we are in some sense stepping out of the world in which we usually live. At least, we should feel as if this is what we are doing. So we need to fix a regular exit point in the onward rush of our day. We need to make a time in our day when everything stops (or, perhaps, first thing in the morning, before everything starts), and a quiet, still space in our home, free from external distraction.

And yet, as we shall see, the main distraction is always oneself, the chatter of the mind reassuring itself in the dark. The quiet place we are seeking is an inner stillness, yet to be discovered. It is in support of our search for this place within that we need to create an external space that is uncharted and at the same time protected. How do we do this? The answer is rather traditional. We make it a sacred place, a ritual space.

Meditating with others helps to generate a more powerful ritual space, but you can create your own by setting aside a corner of your home for meditation, and placing there something to suggest the state of mind you are trying to nurture – a picture, a vase of flowers, or whatever. Buddhists meditate in front of a shrine, simple or elaborate. This provides a kind of gateway to the mind, as well as arousing the sense of awe and reverence that comes naturally to all possessors of human consciousness, but that gets lost in the dust of our passing days. The central place on most shrines is devoted to some sort of Buddha image, an image that conveys the point of what one is doing more clearly and immediately than any number of words.

Whether you call yourself a Buddhist or not, sitting in front of a Buddha image (called a rūpa, which means 'form') does not signify that you have turned your life over to some clunking religiosity. Far from being exotic, it points the way home, giving us the space to appreciate those things that are so humdrum we usually don't even see them. It means opening up the gaps between what we usually think of as the main events of the day, finding value in the moments between our practical affairs, jumping the tramlines of our own narrow concerns and discovering that there really is – if we attend to it – a whole world, so to speak, out there.

A Buddha image on a shrine is not an idol. It does not represent some sort of god. It represents the open-endedness of the exploration of the mind and heart, a recognition that there is no limit to that process and that we cannot therefore conceive of where it is leading – or indeed what deeper processes may be going on underneath, whatever sense we are making of it. This perspective is surprisingly practical. If you find yourself losing heart when you don't seem to be getting the results you envisaged, or if you start to get overexcited and lose concentration when you seem to be doing well – and this is bound to happen sometimes – it is important to have a way of shifting your focus beyond short-term goals.

One way to do this is to dedicate the meditation to its unknowable dimension: to offer it to the Buddha, who represents the ideal of what you are trying to do with your life. You are then free to get on with the meditation. You aren't trapped with some rather cramped and superficial mental states, nor are you floating off on inflated fantasies of being on the verge of Enlightenment. Whether it seems to be going well or not, you can relax and just keep putting one foot in front of the other.

It is to encourage this open-ended perspective that Buddhists usually bow to the shrine before meditating, and perhaps offer flowers or incense. Bowing, like chanting verses or mantras, is a simple way of putting yourself, heart and soul, into the meditation practice. And we need to have feeling, even passion, for what we are doing. If our intention to meditate is just an idea, it won't keep us going long; it will be like the kind of New Year's resolution that is forgotten by the middle of January.

Whether you think in terms of connecting with your positive motivation within, or have a sense of invoking the help of a living presence beyond or outside you – and either of these can be expressed through bowing to a shrine – it basically comes down to the same thing. You are calling forth something to take care of your practice that is outside the control of the conceptualizing mind.

You can connect with your inspiration and purpose in other ways, too; by reading a few lines of poetry, say, or bringing to mind someone whose qualities you admire. This needn't be some big-deal Buddhist. You can look at a child banging the floor with a wooden spoon, or scribbling with an orange crayon. Then look for your own innocent pleasure, your own simplicity and absorption. The secret of meditation lies in the preparation. Have a sense that you are dedicating yourself – dedicating this time and this place – to meditation.

3

Coming to Our Senses

Love's mysteries in souls do grow,
But yet the body is his book.

John Donne, 'The Ecstasy'

It may appear that your body is doing nothing much in meditation: you leave it sitting on the ground while your mind gets on with it. However, this is not the way Buddhism works. The Buddhist agenda is not to free up one's true spiritual nature from the trammels of material form. According to Buddhism, mind and body arise in dependence upon each other. They are different categories, not separate realities. Most of the time we treat our bodies just as the apparatus by means of which we experience the world as feeling, react to it as emotion, and work our will upon it as action. It's a sort of go-between, a resource to be used. But in meditation you don't try to concentrate the mind in isolation. Concentration also involves bringing your physical experience together. The body is attended to from within – that is, we begin to occupy it fully, we begin to enjoy being at home in it.

Strange to say, this is not where we usually are. Our normal experience of life is a sort of out-of-body experience. We are elsewhere. We have a wonderful capacity to check out of our present situation and try out others in our imagination, and sometimes we use that as a sort of escape mechanism. If we are not altogether present, this is generally because we don't want to be. We don't want to feel all our feelings, or express all our emotions.

We don't really escape them, however. They are registered unconsciously in the body, and manifest as tension in certain areas – the jaw, perhaps, or the hands, the hips, or the stomach. This tension blocks the flow of energy to other areas and results in various forms of stiffness or slackness of gait and posture. The English language recognizes this close connection between states of mind and states of body with expressions like 'heartless', 'stiff-necked', and 'cold feet'. Our body shape changes from day to day depending on our mood and general state of mind, and as we grow older it bears clearer traces of our personality and our approach to life. In this way our mental states become embodied.

All this is simply to say that the mind and the body constitute the two ends of a single process, and that we can start to change ourselves through the body as well as through the mind. The focusing of ourselves that the Buddhist tradition calls mindfulness involves a focus of posture as well as of mind; it is also 'bodyfulness' (and 'heartfulness'). So the first task in meditation is to release tension, to relax, and to open up the body. That will help the thoughts and feelings associated with those tensions to emerge gradually into consciousness.

You may like to do a little physical exercise before you meditate – a few yoga stretches or ch'i-kung exercises, say – to begin the process of entering into your physical experience. Then find a good meditation posture – one that embodies the state of mind you intend to cultivate. It will be secure and stable, but also comfortable and responsive, relaxed and energetic. Think of someone carrying a pitcher of water on her head. The energy of the body is unified, focused, bringing a natural dignity and strength to the posture. No part of the spine is rigid or slumped.

Sitting cross-legged or kneeling is generally best, supported by cushions or a stool. Adjust the height of the cushions to make sure you can feel the support of the ground through your knees and legs, while at the same time leaving the whole length of your spine free and flexible. You may have to sit with a little physical discomfort to begin with, just as you may have to sit with uncomfortable mental states, but in the long run this sort of posture should prove the easiest to maintain for long periods. Your hands should be supported in some way – perhaps on a blanket folded around you. If you like, you can place one hand in the other, but don't interlock your fingers, as that can lead to the development of tension in the hands. Tilt your chin slightly downwards, to maintain the flow of energy through your neck, while allowing your back and neck to stay relaxed (see p.127).

If you need to sit in a chair, it is best not to lean against the back. Putting a thin piece of wood or a couple of books under the back feet of the chair to tilt it forward a little will take pressure off the base of your spine. Plant both feet firmly on the floor. If you are ill or in pain and need to sit or lie in bed, you can still meditate. Most people, whatever their meditation posture, occasionally experience physical pain in meditation. This can often be relieved just by a little movement. If you have chronic pain, try to find a middle way between pushing the pain out of your awareness and letting it dominate. Try to allow it its place among other aspects of your experience. This is easier said than done, but there are no easy answers in meditation. Meditation is designed to take us beyond the sense-based experience in which pleasure and pain can dominate the mind; but of course pain can seem to hold us in the realm of the senses rather more insistently than physical pleasure. All one can offer is the traditional Buddhist view, which is that pain provides a much stronger motivation to make one's meditation effective.

In my experience, many beginners listen patiently to all these kinds of considerations and then make themselves comfortable leaning against the wall or even lying down. This is unfortunate I think. But it is understandable because the idea that you meditate with your body simply runs counter to some deep-lying contemporary assumptions about the nature of the mind and of reality itself. One is naturally inclined to follow the dictates of these assumptions until one actually tries meditating in a posture that in some way rings true.

To get an impression of the kind of posture you are aiming for, look at an infant sitting up. The back is straight and at the same time soft. The whole body is relaxed yet totally focused on the object of the child's fascinated attention. A child is as deeply rooted as a tree, and reaches up to the world as easily and naturally as a tree's branches reach up to the sun. Above all, the posture is not fixed, but totally alive.

When you have found such a posture, you are ready to begin meditating. Close your eyes, or settle your gaze softly on the floor in front of you (either is fine). Now the main thing to do is simply to sit still, without fidgeting – which can be surprisingly difficult at first. But sitting still at once reduces sensory input – as does closing the eyes, of course – and you are left with an increased awareness of the thoughts and feelings that usually get tangled up in all that input. If the mind is busy, it won't be the only thing. Sitting still, you gradually become aware that the body is never actually still. It consists in constant movement, some obvious, some more subtle.

Surprisingly, perhaps, it can take quite a bit of practice to become really aware of your body. To begin with, you can find yourself sitting atop your physical experience as if it were alien territory. This territory cannot be forcibly reoccupied; you need to approach it not like a business takeover or a military coup, but as you would approach something that requires a great deal of sensitivity – birdwatching, perhaps. Your body is not an object, but your own immediate experience. Looking around your inner world of sense experience, wait for steady, clear sensations to make themselves felt, then experience them just as they are, as sensations.

Most of our raw energy comes from the lower parts of our body, and meditation needs energy. Your posture should therefore carry a sense of belonging to the earth. On this solid base, your torso can rise up with a sense of lightness, buoyancy, spaciousness, a sense that you can take up as much space as you need, that you can fill it with your presence, that there is always room to expand your boundaries. Gradually you experience your body as a single, integrated whole.

Take time over this. Just sitting still helps to create a calmer mental state. Like a still lake, the quiet body offers a mirror to the mind. There is no need to run after your experience, or work anything out, or imagine anything. Don't worry about distractions, just let them be in the background. Normally it is our sense of the body that is in the background, while our thinking swanks about in the foreground, imagining fondly that it is making all the decisions. If your thinking can at least be gradually relegated to the background, that's a good start.

Start around the eyes, as that is where we tend to locate our attention. Notice any clenching or tightness around the eyes, or behind them. Let your attention drop away from behind the eyes towards the back of the head. Notice any clenching in the forehead, and imagine that knot unravelling and opening out along the forehead towards the temples. Let your attention drift up towards the crown of the head, and start to take in the whole of the scalp. Notice the sensations of the ears. Then other parts of the face. Notice particularly any clenching in the cheeks. Let the jaw loosen. Then notice the various different sensations and feelings inside the mouth. The sense of taste at this moment, the saliva, the inside of the cheeks. Notice inside the nostrils, the inbreath, the outbreath. You now have something to hold onto, and you can slowly ride the breath deep into the body, noting the extraordinary range of sensation and feeling in the body, the internal organs with their curious needs – for air, for food, for evacuation, and so on – the duller sensations of muscles, the sense of structure and support from the bones, the intense sensitivity of the skin. The feeling of clothing against the skin. Notice sounds as just another layer of sensation in the body. Notice the body's knowledge of the earth, the sense of the weight of the body meeting the support of the earth. Notice the body's knowledge of the sky, of the infinity of space reaching out in all directions. Notice the body's sense of the world around, including other people.

Just give attention to every corner of your sensory world, from the toes to the scalp, letting go of any tension or dullness, awakening and relaxing your whole body. Bring awareness to your skin, muscles, organs, even your bones. As you do so, your mind will also begin to relax and come alive.

4

You Are
Already Aware

*The 'I think' which Kant said must be able to accompany all
my objects is the 'I breathe' which actually does accompany
them.*

William James, *Radical Empiricism*

We all, from time to time, find ourselves with nothing to do. We
look for some object to stimulate our interest, but nothing does.
This is meditation's arena, its building site. Boredom. One of the
most worrying developments of recent decades is the elimination
of boredom. Boredom is the cradle of creativity and awareness.

Cutting off our usual distractions, we take an interest in *what
we want to distract ourselves from*. Is the mind left to itself simply
nothing, an unused piece of equipment, or is it perhaps the
missing piece of the jigsaw of our life?

To begin with you may not know what you are really supposed
to be doing with this unoccupied time. Eventually, you will start
to become more familiar with the overall medium in which you
are working. This medium is awareness, and the ingredients
with which you work are the ever-changing objects that come

into your awareness. Sitting still you become aware that most of these objects of awareness are uninvited; you do not choose to think of, say, what you are going to have for breakfast – but suddenly *you become aware that this is what you are thinking about*. As an example of awareness this may not seem like much, but actually it represents an amazingly powerful process if you can only harness it. It is the process of waking up to your life. The question is: how do you deliberately cultivate this haphazard occurrence of awareness? How can you deliberately wake up?

The simple answer is to stop, just stop and be still. And then pay attention. Before applying a meditation technique, it is important to establish this basic procedure as where we start and where we end in meditation. Specific meditation practices will help you to be more at home with this experience and to explore its possibilities in different ways, but, when in doubt about what you are doing, 'stop and look' is always a useful principle to fall back on.

When leading meditations I tend to avoid the expression 'Be aware' as in 'Be aware of the feeling in your tongue.' This is to avoid reinforcing the notion that awareness is willed into existence. Our thinking tends to assume control of everything, including awareness, but this is a case of the lunatics taking over the asylum. I think it is more useful to imagine that awareness is already there in one's immediate physical experience. All we have to do is unify it. Pay attention to it. Take an interest in it. Be mindful.

One would be forgiven for thinking that mindfulness is the mind becoming aware of the body. But it is more like the body becoming aware of the mind.

Part Two

Mindfulness

5

What Is Mindfulness?

*The secret motive of the absent-minded is to be innocent
while guilty.*

Saul Bellow, *More Die of Heartbreak*

Reasons to be mindful

Like any animal we operate as a stimulus-response programme,
so most of the time we don't give our attention at all – it is taken
by stealth. We very rarely make a choice to look at advertisements
for example. They just 'grab' you, as do all sorts of objects we are
attracted to or repelled by. The world has this power over us. It
locks onto our emotional circuits, setting off repetitive patterns
of thinking.

A thought arises without you being aware of it. You then,
still subconsciously, scan the thought and react to it in some
emotionally based way. Identifying with the thought then
happens automatically: you are not aware of the thought as a
thought. You are now on what the great mindfulness teacher,
Jon Kabat Zinn, calls 'automatic pilot'. Most of this thinking is

'negative'. The brain is a wonderful problem-solving organ, so it naturally focuses on the negative. That's its job – some bit of us has to do it. However, this background thinking gives our experience its taste, which is more or less bitter or flavourless.

Awareness gives us choice, and thus enables us to improve our experience, but the possibilities for improvement are endless, so our thinking is too. We avoid fully experiencing a present reality that is inevitably less than completely satisfying, in favour of a semi-conscious inner life of thinking and fantasy. This makes our experience even less satisfactory and drives us to seek further distractions from it, thus perpetuating and deepening the problem. Our unlived life rots away in the mind, and congeals in the body, poisoning and deadening what should be the miracle of being alive. We become restless and discontented.

So our wonderful individuality, our self-awareness, turns into a kind of phantom self, existing on a purely mental level, made up of ideas of its past and its future and the ideas of it given to us by others. We spend our entire lives catering to the literally endless demands of this phantom self. It becomes our central reality. We become trapped in our compulsive thinking. We appropriate our experience in a constant stream of endlessly reheated thoughts – we are quite literally 'selfish'. In the end, all our experience tastes the same, it has the same 'me' flavour – in other words, it is all 'my' experience. It is as if our self-concern exudes a constant bitter flavouring agent, made up of our thinking. It is as if we hear everything against a constant roar of mindless thoughts, as if we see everything through a thick veil of our own needs and fears.

As it is the only reality we know, we don't see this as being as bad as I have made it seem. Indeed, most of us manage to live pretty cheerful lives. We are a resilient and adaptable species. We are able to alleviate the symptoms of our condition in all sorts of ways with work, friends, family, exercise, art, religion, psychotherapy, and so on. However, the Buddha's teaching is designed to address the underlying issue that I have sketched out in this section, an issue traditionally called saṃsāra (literally, the going on and on of things). The Buddha offers a way to be free of saṃsāra. But this involves becoming more and more familiar with its harsh music, how and where its individual notes are being produced at this very moment, and on that basis how we can bring our life in closer harmony with how things really are.

Meditation 'objects' or supports, and how to use them

for the roses
Had the look of flowers that are looked at.

T.S. Eliot, 'Burnt Norton'

Meditation practices are designed to develop qualities of mind that, to some extent, we already possess. They do this through deliberately connecting what we are doing at any moment with what we are doing the next. This makes us aware of the conflicts that make our experience so disconnected, and this awareness of itself has the power to resolve those conflicts.

The first aim of any meditation technique is to develop a continuous flow of positive mental states. The key word here is 'continuous'. Everyone has positive mental states from time to time – we all know what it is to be happy, content, joyful, kind, and generous. Meditation involves consciously sustaining a continuous flow of such positive states. So the starting point of meditation is to become aware of the flow of what is going on in the mind – whether positive or negative – so that we can learn to direct that flow.

The problem is that it is difficult to work on the quality of our awareness directly. Awareness by its nature cannot be known as an object of awareness. It is knowing. All we get is a reflection of its quality in the feelings provoked by the objects that come before it.

This leads us to a crucial error, because certain objects in certain contexts (ice cream, say) are guaranteed to deliver superficially pleasant feelings whatever the quality of our awareness may be. As a result, instead of cultivating the *quality* of our awareness, we cultivate the *objects* of our awareness. That is, we seek pleasure rather than awareness or understanding. Meditation is designed to reverse this process – so we give the mind an object like the breathing, or a mantra, say, that acts as a mirror, or a reference point, to draw it together.

If we think of meditation as an experience we want to have, we won't get far. We will just be persisting in our habitual strategy in life, which is to focus on experiences that press our reward buttons, and to ignore or flinch from those that don't. Meditation does not just deliver another experience. It runs a thread of awareness through them. We may have all sorts of wonderful – or occasionally unsettling – experiences while we are meditating, but meditation itself is the activity of connecting up our experience into what we call awareness.

Mindfulness is not a forced concentration, but it is something deliberate. It is a deliberate gathering of attention, a drawing together of all one's faculties. It is an intentional awareness, a directed attentiveness. It involves being aware of what has happened, being watchful for what may be about to happen, and being true to one's purpose.

Mindfulness literally means remembering. You are remembering to be aware, to pay attention. Awareness is about taking in what's going on as it is going on. It is essentially *receptive*, while mindfulness is the *activity* of bringing awareness into being. Mindfulness is the monitoring process in meditation, remembering what you are doing. It is like a sheepdog gathering sheep in a field and driving them into a sheepfold. Or like a tiger stalking its prey. Focused and flexible. But also receptive, ears pricked.

Concentration in meditation is not an exercise in fixation. Awareness does not isolate its object from its context. Above all, it must include the *subject* of awareness – you. Whether you are focusing on an external object or mental image, or on some other thought, feeling, or sensation, that context includes you, a sense of yourself being there, an awareness of your general mental state, and especially your physical presence. You need to be aware of the object from within your own body, so to speak.

You become aware not just of objects, but of objects being attended to. Try to 'take in' the object before you, to *acknowledge* what you are taking in. If you can 'give yourself' to the object of your awareness, this enables the object, whatever it is – whether a flower or your own mental state – to speak more clearly to you. Your attention to the object needs to settle very gently on it, to catch the fresh taste of this moment.

You become aware that what you are looking at, hearing, smelling, tasting, feeling, or thinking is being looked at, heard, smelt, tasted, felt or thought about. It's that simple. In fact, you can start now; not later, when you've bought a meditation cushion or when the children have grown up. Now. Be aware that you are reading this.

The object in mindfulness or meditation is there to trigger the recollecting process, not force it. You cannot *force* yourself to remember. The key to concentration in meditation is to relax your attention, and then remember to come back to the object. Rest your attention almost casually on the object. When you realize that your mind has wandered, that is remembering. Well done, you're doing it! Now you can just come back to the object nice and slow and easy.

'Taste the day'

It is at this point that people say, 'I'm fine with attending to what is going on in the present moment. But how do you keep it going?' This is a good question, because it exposes a common confusion in meditation between ends and means. It also exposes that part of us, the controlling, judgemental part of us, which resists the whole project. Yes the goal is to master the mind, but the means to do so is to take a kindly interest in it, not to try to master it. The simple answer to the question is, 'You only ever have to do the practice now. So what is going on now? Notice the anxiety to control, to get on top of the exercise.'

Notice too the 'good' part of the mind trying to pin down the 'slack' part into doing what it doesn't really want to do. That splitting of the mind, the ability to reflect on ourselves, is a necessary stage in the development of awareness. But mindfulness is about bringing the mind together again. So don't try to control the mind; it wanders because it is not fully engaged; and you need that desire for engagement: by wishing your busy mind away you are also wishing away your interest and engagement.

Mindfulness is really not so much about being in the now as about bringing together emotional energies. 'Being in the now' is a popular idea, but it is just a useful way of speaking. It shouldn't be taken literally. Everything you do, even thinking about the past or the future, takes place in the present moment anyway. The Latin poet Horace is known for one expression above all others: 'carpe diem', usually translated as 'seize the day.' However, the modern poet Harry Eyres suggests that a better translation in the context of that particular ode is 'taste the day.' Which is a good way of describing mindfulness because of its sensuousness.

One thing you should notice about your sensations is that they are very different. Some are strong, others are quite soft-focus. Some are pleasant, others less so. And you inevitably pick and choose between these elements of your experience. Now you might say, well, of course you do. You want agreeable experiences, and you want to avoid disagreeable ones. But let's look at this. Actually we want to avoid setting up conditions that will deliver disagreeable experiences. Once an experience is there, whether agreeable or not, it is unavoidable. It is the doomed attempt to avoid painful feeling that has already arrived that is the source of our suffering.

The aim is to be in a sense whole. To be all there. To be present. This is in fact a much more counter-intuitive objective than it seems. We probably take up meditation in order to leave behind our stressful, busy, anxious experience of ourselves and find calm, peace, even happiness. That is, we want only part of our experience, the nice part.

Our problems arise out of trying to not experience the difficult bits. We *say* we'd like to live in the present moment, but it's always in the context of some idyllic situation. Being in the present involves also being present with difficult experience. Or rather it is about being present with the mix of pleasant and difficult.

Say, for instance, that someone says something unkind to me. To avoid the painful feeling I may perhaps react with anger. Strong emotion like this is analgesic. It is a way of not feeling the pain. There are all sorts of other ways of avoiding the experience of difficult feeling – eating, drinking alcohol, smoking. Any distraction is an avoidance mechanism. But, as we have seen, the feeling isn't avoided – it just gets locked in the body. So being present, mindfulness, begins in the body, especially with uncomfortable feeling.

Mindfulness of feeling is about not adding anything to our experience. Taking on our experience just as it is, and seeing if we can just drop the fuss we make about it.

Oddly, however, we also tend not to notice pleasant feeling. Partly because it is more or less ever-present – like the breathing.

We take it for granted. There is a famous story of a Zen student who complained to his teacher that he found practising awareness of the breathing boring. The Zen master did not reply. He just dragged the student to the nearby river and held his head under the water. After a minute or so, he pulled the boy's head up. As the first fiercely rasping breaths were being taken, the master said mildly, 'How boring is the breath now?'

The same goes for other sensory experience. If you are distracted by noise, for example, notice your hearing, the fact that you hear. Seeing too is a deeply pleasurable experience. The basic pleasure of art is just the joy of looking for the sake of looking.

The modern composer John Cage was one day exiting a particular exhibition of paintings, when he discovered that he was deriving precisely the same aesthetic appreciation from looking at the pavement as he had from looking at the paintings. That is, his eyes had been opened. And this is the function of his own work, his music – to open the ears, to awaken our hearing. He did this in a very uncompromising way. His most famous – or notorious – piece, called '4 minutes 33 seconds', is for piano, and it consists in complete silence, divided into three sections by the raising and lowering of the piano lid. The audience largely missed the point, which was that the silence was not silence at all. There was no *intentional* sound – as with conventional music – but, as Cage observed later, there was still plenty to hear. During the first movement there was the sound of wind outside, during the second section rain drops fell on the roof, and in the third section there were the 'interesting sounds' of people talking and walking out.

The piece was apparently inspired by a visit to an anechoic chamber, a completely soundproofed room. When he emerged from it, Cage complained to the technicians that he had heard two quite distinct sounds, one high-pitched, the other low-pitched. It was explained to him that the sounds were his nervous system and his blood circulating.

For Cage, music arises from an attitude of mind that does not pick and choose. By giving his interested attention to all the irritating 'noises' that modern urban life served up to him, he came to actively enjoy the sound of traffic and even the hum of the refrigerator as genuinely beautiful. His work sought to communicate not so much an experience as an attitude to experience. As with other examples of modern art, the mind and senses of the listener or viewer provide an essential part of the work. Faced with what appears to be nothing much at all, we start to get glimpses of a world of magic and riches. This world is always available to us. A friend of mine who was once a student of John Cage's used to say that the most beautiful sound he ever heard was John Cage dragging a table across the floor.

There is one more thing to notice about your present experience. This is that your sensations (and feelings), whether pleasant or difficult, are always changing. You may direct your attention to, say, your feet, to your left big toe, but then you should start to see the difference between the words 'left big toe' and your actual experience of it. You start to see that your experience is ungraspable, and that in the end this goes for all our experience, whether pleasant or difficult.

6

The Mindfulness of Breathing

Like a long-legged fly upon the stream
His mind moves upon silence.

W.B. Yeats, 'Long-legged fly'

The most widely practised mindfulness meditation in the Buddhist tradition is the Mindfulness of Breathing. There are various reasons for the importance of this practice. Breathing is deeply and subtly enjoyable. It is the most fundamental experience of being alive. It is where we connect with the outside world most immediately. Each breath we take is a reminder that our life is on loan. Every few moments we are given a refreshing new lungful of air to enjoy. At the same time we are always letting go of the breath, and one day we will let go of it for the last time.

The breath also reveals how the mind connects with the body – as when, say, we hold the breath, or release it slowly while performing some delicate task. The breath is where we connect with our feelings and emotions most directly – when our breathing quickens, when we gasp or even stop breathing momentarily, when we laugh or whistle or sing.

We often 'take a deep breath' to collect ourselves before doing something challenging, and this is quite a good way to start the Mindfulness of Breathing. Once you have settled yourself down to meditate and brought your awareness to your physical experience, just take a few deep breaths to bring your breathing into the general frame of your attention.

After that, just allow your breathing to be natural. The meditation involves attending to the breath, not trying to control it or do anything with it. Your body will reach for each breath by itself. Just let it come and go in its own time, while keeping it steadily in mind.

I suspect that a lot of the difficulties people have with meditation practice revolve around not trusting the power of awareness. It feels counter-intuitive to trust awareness, to have faith in just being conscious, without trying to exert some conscious control. Breathing happens on its own, whether we notice it or not. But unlike other essential processes that the body carries out for itself, it can also be consciously controlled. In this practice we aim to be conscious of the breathing *but not to control it in any way*. If, as part of the practice, we can notice any tendency to try to control the breath, this gives us an interesting sense of the way the mind tries to control our experience when we have set out only to be aware of it. Don't worry: as you continue to practise, the mind will naturally loosen its grip on what it is prepared to experience.

The practice is usually divided into several stages. The following version has four. Allow about five minutes for each stage when you're learning the meditation.

The first stage

In the first stage of the practice, you number each outbreath. After an outbreath, count 'one' (mentally, not out loud). After the next breath count 'two', and so on, until you have counted ten breaths. Then go back to 'one' and count ten breaths again, and so on. If you lose count, or realize that you have counted beyond ten, just start again at 'one'.

The counting is useful because it gives you early warning of the mind wandering – you will be aware of losing count before you are aware of having drifted off – as well as an instant yardstick for your initial attention span. In themselves, the numbers are not an important part of the practice; they just pin your attention to the breath until you can maintain some continuity of awareness without them. So keep the counting quite muted (or if you are more of a visualizer, introduce the numbers unobtrusively in the corner of the 'canvas'). The breath is the star of the show – indeed, you can attend to the breath as if you were listening to music. Don't try to control your breathing – just let it go its own way and follow it.

Nor is there any need to worry about the mind wandering. It will wander. You could imagine that you have tethered your mind as you would a goat in the middle of a field. You allow it plenty of rope so that it can wander about, but all the time you are gently drawing it in. The challenge is to bring your attention back to the breathing as soon as you realize it has wandered away. That is what mindfulness is. At the same time, see if you can feel the breath creating a sense of space and light in which any tangles of tension, impatience, or dullness may loosen and dissolve.

The second stage

In the second stage, count before each inbreath: 'one' (breathe in, breathe out), 'two' (breathe in, breathe out), and so on, up to 'ten', then start again at 'one'. That is to say, anticipate what is going to happen instead of marking what has already happened. This change is subtle, but it reflects quite an important shift. In fact, subtle though it is, it tells us something crucial about the nature of awareness. One could even say that truly ethical behaviour has its basis in this kind of shift – the shift from being aware that something has happened to being aware that it is about to happen. Awareness after the event – after you have reacted to something – is a start: it's the beginning of mindfulness. But the aim is to catch the impulse in the mind before it is translated into speech or action. Then, finally, you are in the driving seat: your actions are your own and you are taking responsibility for them.

But you still don't go chasing after the breath. It's more like you are looking out for it as it gradually emerges at the centre of your attention, while around it is a general awareness of the whole body. From time to time it may be obscured by distractions, but these are like clouds passing across the sky of the mind. The breath is always there behind them, like the sun behind the clouds, and your body is relaxed and alive, and immovable as a mountain. Clouds will always tend to form around mountains, and storms will beat about you in that rarefied atmosphere. But don't let the clouds – the distractions – discourage you. Implicit in the awareness of being in a negative mental state is the seed of its opposite. Look for the stillness at the heart of your awareness of being restless.

The third stage

Now fade out the counting altogether. You may find that you are sufficiently present – your energies sufficiently integrated – for just sitting with the breath to be very satisfying in itself, and that is the aim of this stage. You just feel the breath coming and going like the waves of the sea. You don't watch it, you are aware of it – your awareness is with it, within it. Welcome each moment in with the breath, and see it out again. Feel your belly drawing energy up with the breath. Allow your chest and shoulders to open as the tide of the breath turns.

This stage is traditionally said to be like watching a child on a swing: there is a feeling of pleasure tempered with care and watchfulness. Try to get a sense of the breath as a whole, as it moves through the cycle of inhalation and exhalation. Feel the movement of the whole torso. Pay particular attention to the turn of the breath – this is where you are most likely to lose concentration. Experiment with allowing your attention to deepen and broaden. If you drift off, draw your attention back to the breath. Focus in the breath, rather than on it.

The fourth stage

In the final stage of the meditation, focus on a small detail of the breathing process: the point where you experience the breath entering or leaving your body, usually a subtle flow of sensation around the nostrils. This is quite tricky: the mind has to ride the constantly changing flow of sensation with a very delicate touch. You can't grab at it or hold on to it; when you try, it's already gone. It is always going and all you can do is let it go. But you can't afford to allow your attention to waver for a moment. You have to be absolutely relaxed, and at the same time completely attentive. You release the mind, and at the same time engage it more closely. The breath is now hardly felt as an object at all. You cannot separate yourself from it; you are within it, absorbed in it.

The traditional image for this stage is using a saw on a bit of wood. Your attention is on the point where the moving saw cuts into the wood, just as, with this practice, your attention is on the point where the breath passes a fixed point. It is an image of the mind settling in the midst of changing experience.

Ending the meditation

At the end of the meditation you naturally have to disengage from the breath and allow other things to come to your attention. Take your time with this transition; plan your time so that you don't have to leap up and rush away to do something else. And try to stay with a sense of being concentrated, fully present, attentive, alert to your purpose. If you meditate in the morning, try to wear the fragrance of your meditation throughout the day. This is as important as the meditation practice itself, and why meditators usually try to slow down and simplify their lives: to find the space to be aware.

The Mindfulness of Breathing seems a simple enough exercise, and may sound rather a dull one. But it is not really an activity of such paint-drying monotony. If we attend to it carefully and closely, we find that the breath is never the same experience; it is always new, always changing. And it turns out not to be like mental press-ups because it is not really about watching the breath. It is about watching the mind, watching oneself. Meditation gradually makes it vividly apparent that our experience is not some kind of objective process. We create it. When we think we are experiencing something, what we are really experiencing is – in a sense – ourselves. So the breath is not really an 'object' at all. The breath is also the mind.

Further notes on the Mindfulness of Breathing

I have said that the counting is not important in itself. This does not mean that it should be abandoned if it seems to make the practice more difficult. The practice is not really meant to be easy. A fundamental mistake that beginners make sometimes is to think that meditation should not feel stressful. But sitting with the truth of who or how you are – even if it is just a vague sense of muddle and indecisiveness – must feel a bit uncomfortable sometimes. I know some teachers who say, 'If you don't find the counting helpful, leave it out.' I would say, if the counting makes the exercise more uncomfortable, then persist with it – something is working.

Bear in mind that your attention will naturally tend to drift off when it is directed towards an object like the breath, which does not offer clear conceptual content. The counting provides a little conceptual crutch.

The counting also engages the controlling, anxious side of the mind in the practice. To begin with, it may dominate the whole procedure, a heavy-handed grid of numbers blocked out over the ungraspable immeasurable reality of the breath. It is quite literally the rational, judgemental side of the mind trying to contain our inspiration, our appreciative enjoyment of being alive, breathing. Now it might seem like a good idea just to take a holiday from the dead hand of the rational controlling mind, and leave out the counting. But then the two sides of us never get to work together.

The rational mind needs to partake in the feast of life. Otherwise in the end the excluded rational mind turns demonic. Buddhist meditation is about integrating our experience. It is about becoming whole. If you persist with it, the counting will take its proper place within the larger world of the breath. The rational mind will serve the larger reality of the playful, appreciative, boundary-less mind, the mind that does not attempt to be useful, or to get something out of this moment with the world, with myself, with others.

We should not confuse the view of the rational mind operating on its own with objective truth. The difference between the first stage and the second stage of the practice is meant to drive home the extraordinary subjectivity of the rational mind. Objectively, there is no difference between the two stages – we count the breaths at the same point, between the outbreath and the inbreath, in each stage.

If we simply inserted a word like, say, 'boot' between the breaths, there would be no need to have two separate stages. But a number has to refer to either the previous breath or the following breath. The result is to insert a very basic sense of narrative into the breathing. This reproduces a tendency in the mind to take in its experience in temporal terms, as a story, as emerging from the future and disappearing into the past. In the first stage you become aware of the breath as something that has happened. In the second stage it becomes suddenly something that is about to happen.

I've talked about the importance of being more in the present moment. However, the experience of the present moment, at least at some level, is properly connected to the experience of the past and the future. There is no present without past and future. In music, for example, the beauty of a single note is in its relation to what precedes and follows it. Likewise, our experience of the present moment is coloured by our feeling about the past and our feeling about the future. You may notice that one stage feels easier than the other for this reason. How does it feel to let go of the past moment? How does it feel to welcome in the next moment?

The basic instruction is not to control the breath. But as always in meditation there are two sides to the exercise. You try to do it right, to do what you are supposed to do – in this case, try not to control the breath. But you do so in order to experience more clearly what is actually happening – which in this case may be that you are, willy-nilly, controlling the breath. You can also find yourself anticipating the next number. Or else marking yourself down for getting distracted. And, as always, the secret is to take an interest in what would normally be frustrating.

Most people are looking for an experience of some kind in meditation. Actually the goal is a particular quality of attention, a way of being with one's experience, whatever that experience may be. And this is quite a radical shift in values. It is an opening up of the mind, a containing, accommodating attention. This takes us to the third stage of the practice.

Here, as we become more fully engaged with present experience, we shift from a temporal into a more spatial awareness. And again we start looking for a shape or structure to our experience, this time a spatial structure. However, while there is a general attention to the breath, there is no particular focus, no central point to be found upon which to fix the attention. Nor, when we explore the experience of the breath, do we find a boundary to the breath. While we are aware of the breath we cannot exclude anything from it. We start to experience noises, for example, as simply another layer of sensation around the breath. Wherever the mind goes, we are there with the breath. Of course, the mind looks for something to hold onto, to secure itself upon, but this stage of the practice is about looking for something fixed in our experience and not finding it.

Finally, in the fourth stage, we allow ourselves a focus. I know that some teachers again say that it doesn't matter where you focus, that, if focusing on the tip of the nostrils feels too heady, you can focus on the belly, say, the hara (the deep abdomen, about 5cm below the navel, halfway between front and back), instead. But I think that focusing on the hara has a somewhat different purpose from the last stage of the Mindfulness of Breathing. Here, the aim is to have the clearest sensation possible, which, even when the breath is very subtle, is to be found at this point. If you feel heady, then you can just return to the previous stage. But the idea here I believe is to concentrate the mind around something absolutely clear and absolutely ungraspable. In this stage we are breaking down the dualism of the mind, the attention, as something separate from the body, the breathing. By locating the focus of our attention in the head, we challenge ourselves to experience the head as being not separate from the body.

7

Everyday Mindfulness

If you want to find the meaning, stop chasing after so many things.

Ryōkan, *One Robe, One Bowl*

Mindfulness is cultivated in meditation, but it is more generally practised in everyday life. The result is a deeply fulfilling experience of even the simplest activities. The Zen tradition approaches the goal of Buddhism very much in this way:

How wonderful, how miraculous.
I chop wood, I carry water.

This kind of quiet miracle is perhaps most accessible to us in the peace and spaciousness of nature. But we could just as well cry out, 'How wonderful, how miraculous. I catch the bus home, I make the kids' tea.' Mindfulness brings a depth of colour, resonance, and meaning to life, wherever you are, whatever you are doing, and whatever is happening, whether banal or dramatic.

The idea is not to start trying to squeeze quiet miracles out of everyday activities, but simply to attend to your experience. And when we have a little space, we can allow ourselves to be spacious – not just fill the space with vague, half-conscious distractions. Mindfulness is about remembering, coming back to ourselves, returning to our purpose, and setting up the conditions in which awareness will deepen. We are gradually moving from an awareness that is triggered more or less accidentally to one that is self-generating.

One way to start this process is to keep a diary: you then naturally start to notice more. You can also decide that every time you walk through a doorway, or go up or down stairs, or hear the church bells, you will use that experience to remind yourself to be aware. When you hear the telephone ringing, you can remember your connection with other people and resolve to pay attention to the quality of your communication before you pick up the receiver. You have to be determined to keep trying to make these connections – it's all too easy to forget for days at a time – but, with practice, anything that happens regularly in your life can be turned into a wake-up call.

A traditional Buddhist exercise is to verbalize your awareness, to say to yourself, 'Holding the warm cup . . . sipping the tea . . . thinking about lunch . . . putting the cup down . . . turning to the book again . . . here, now, this.' More precisely, the practice is to attend to the sensations just as sensations. You get behind the label to the actual experience, thus: hard sensation on lip, hot liquid, warm in throat, pleasure, thinking, sound, thinking. . . The verbalization is just a tool, of course, and the less intrusive it is, the more awareness you can bring to what you are doing. It's important not to get too precious about everyday mindfulness if one is to avoid turning it into an exercise in alienation. It shouldn't become a cold mental clamp on our experience. But it is a very useful practice in cultivating a radical shift in emphasis – from valuing particular kinds of experience to valuing an acute and intimate awareness of experience.

Mindfulness involves protecting yourself from distractions; but bear in mind that it can be quite contagious. Do not underestimate the power of mindfulness on others, or the effect that others who practise mindfulness can have on you. The best support for your practice, as Buddhists down the ages have always recognized, is regular contact with others who also practise mindfulness.

In some ways mindfulness outside meditation is very different from – although related to – mindfulness within it. Instead of the mind responding to its own processes, the self is responding to the world, particularly in terms of behaviour. As you become more conscious that your experience always contains two poles – subject and object, self and other – you start to appreciate that it always consists of relationship.

Our experience is not just to be consumed; it is to be listened to – for at every moment something is being asked of us. Mindfulness involves an appreciation of whatever we do and whoever we meet – however difficult or straightforward we may find that situation – as giving us something to work with. It means attending to small details, respecting the simple commodities of existence – a chair, toast and butter, tea, appetite. It connects the world we know, neatly packaged like this book, with the world we don't know, the one that is happening. Meditation is a vital training for the mind, but what it is working with in the end is the relationship between the self and the world. The transformation of the mind is the transformation of that relationship.

Walking meditation

> *When I walk alone in the beautiful orchard, if my thoughts*
> *have been dwelling on extraneous incidents for a while, I*
> *bring them back to the walk, to the orchard, to the sweetness*
> *of this solitude, and to me.*

Michel de Montaigne, *Essays*

The Buddhist tradition of walking meditation has its origin in the Buddha's teaching that one should always try to be aware of what one is doing – standing, sitting, walking, or lying down. This most basic level of mindfulness may sound like something we naturally do already, but in practice we all have the experience of somehow having moved from a to b without having noticed we have done so. One minute you're sitting in front of the television, the next you're in the kitchen putting the kettle on, and you have no idea how you got there. It is as if something beyond our control is making our decisions for us.

So any simple, especially rhythmic, activity can be made into a meditative practice, for example washing up, ironing, and particularly walking. Instead of mentally 'checking out' of what we are doing, and letting the mind drift aimlessly from one thing to another, we deliberately attend to the moment-by-moment details of our experience as they come to us.

Meditation is associated with being still, but what you notice when you are still is that there is movement in the body all the time. The stillness is mobile, even lively. Walking meditation has basically the same quality of stillness to it as sitting meditation.

You walk quite slowly, limiting visual input by focusing on the ground in front of you. As traditionally practised, the walking has no destination, no purpose beyond itself. A Zen teacher has described it as being like carefully sewing a robe, each footstep a finely judged stitch. This beautiful image emphasizes an important aesthetic dimension to this practice. It connects our mindfulness practice to the world of our everyday activities, and in doing so gathers our ragged experience of the world into a beautiful sustained presence.

Instead of the walking being a chore to get through, it becomes something we do for its own sake. It gets us into the habit of making the details of ordinary life something to savour for their own sake. It also extends the practice of concentration: we can alternate sitting and walking practice.

The practice is to anchor the mind in some particular aspect of the immediate physical experience of walking as it is happening, for instance the breath or the footsteps. Both of these details are easy to notice. They also offer a way into a deeper mindfulness. So if you are busy or in a hurry, just notice these aspects of your experience in the background, as something to earth what you are doing in a sense of being present, aware. Notice the rhythm of the breath. Notice the rhythm of the footsteps.

If you have less business to occupy yourself, start to notice *this* footstep. Leave the rhythm of the breath in the background. And now *this* footstep. As with the breath, a single experience breaks down under examination into a flow of different sensations. Get into the details: as the leg swings forward notice the heel searching for the resistance of the ground. Then notice it meeting the ground and pinning your weight to the earth, and notice your momentum carrying your weight over the heel and onto the ball of the foot, the whole of your weight pinning itself to the earth through heel, ball, and toes as the other foot swings forward. Notice the sensations of muscle, joint, and bone moving, balancing, taking weight. Bring conscious attention to other details of the experience of walking in this way. Notice the feelings in the left ankle, tendons, and calf muscles as they flex and release. Then notice the feelings in the right leg.

Bring attention into the movement as it is taking place rather than simply noticing that it has taken place. It is about coming into the *experience* as it is, rather than into the *idea* of it. Eventually you will be present with the whole body as it moves moment by moment, even while you bring a gentle but penetrating focus on particular aspects of it.

There are other aspects of your experience you can take in as you walk: the sensation of clothes against the skin. Temperature:

take in the coolness of some parts of the body, the warmth of others. Notice sounds: let the labelling process fade into the background and bring forward the sound that the moment carries to you. Savour the impermanence of it. Be aware not only of what you hear, but also of the hearing itself. Notice the thought that has turned up in your mind. Notice its emotional tone.

Make a point of limiting what you take in visually. At some point you may decide to pay mindful attention to your visual field, but it is very easy to lose awareness completely when we allow the visual world to pull us this way and that. However, just for short periods initially, practise being mindful of visual objects; again let the labelling process be in the background as far as possible; notice colours, shapes, textures, qualities of light and shade, all shifting and changing as you move among them.

Slow walking
Gradually slow down your walking, becoming more aware of the breathing, noticing the syncopation of its rhythm against that of the footsteps, until you can time the footsteps to match the breathing, breathing in and out during one footstep. Bring the foot up with the inbreath. Bring it down with the outbreath. Let your natural breathing lead the footsteps, rather than timing the footsteps to the breathing.

Planting meditation
This practice comes from the great modern teacher Thich Nhat Hanh.

Imagine that with each step you are planting a seed in the earth. A seed of awareness, or of kindness, or of patience. Make it what you like. But be clear about what it is you are planting.

You are planting the seed in the world, to grow and fructify there. But you are also planting the seed in your own mind, where you can imagine that it will grow.

The point of this practice is that it is a *seed* you are planting. So it doesn't matter if you don't experience the quality at this moment. What you do have is sufficient awareness to know that the quality is not present, or not present to the extent you would like it to be. That is the seed. An awareness of the absence of any desired internal object, whether an image or a positive quality of mind, is the seed of its presence. With time this seed will fructify. In the end this planting of seeds becomes a sense of simply walking in peace in the world.

Part Three

Kindness

8

Mettā

While on the shop and street I gazed
My body of a sudden blazed;
And twenty minutes more or less
It seemed, so great my happiness,
That I was blessed and could bless.

W.B. Yeats, 'Vacillation'

The cultivation of emotions

The Mettā Bhāvanā, the development of universal loving-kindness, is as fundamental a meditation practice as the Mindfulness of Breathing. Here, though, the object of attention is the flow, not of the breath, but of the emotions. And we don't just attend to the emotions; we actively cultivate certain emotions in particular.

So how do we feel about cultivating emotions? The very idea seems artificial. We want to be authentic. Of course we do. And authenticity is an important emotion to cultivate.

I think the point here is that we do cultivate emotions anyway, just not very consciously. We cultivate emotions with our thoughts and words, with our choices of behaviour, with the views we hold. If, for example, I think or say 'that is so unreasonable' and stomp off slamming the door, and if I hold the view that it is reasonable to expect people to be reasonable, then I am cultivating a certain emotion (in this case, anger).

We often use the words 'feeling' and 'emotion' as though they mean the same thing, but, when it comes to meditation, it is important to distinguish between them. We cannot choose our feelings: we have no choice whether something that happens to us produces a pleasant or an unpleasant feeling. But emotion is different. It is an action – the action of making something of one's feelings. For example, to walk out of a warm house into the bitter wind of a winter's day may feel unpleasant, and you can't do anything about that. But reactions like tensing yourself up against the cold and grumbling that you hate winter, or snapping out of it and trying to be positive, clearly involve some element of choice. Indeed, if you can be a little more sensitive and aware, you can perhaps come up with more interesting emotional options than either of these. You can notice the physical tensing up, the mind getting surly, the wind sighing, a couple of small birds hopping about on a bare branch, other people looking tense and surly . . . and then your shoulders relaxing, your mood lightening momentarily.

The Mettā Bhāvanā involves caring about the way one responds to the world. It is the cultivation not of feelings but of emotions, not of experiences but of actions – because our choices of action are initially made at an emotional level. So one has to stop confusing feeling with emotion, or at least recognize that there are two processes going on in any emotional 'experience'. Meditation helps to separate out these processes by slowing everything down, taking our experience frame by frame.

Because we don't tend to experience emotion separately from feeling, we rarely identify emotions as matters of choice: they blur into the area of feelings, where we have no choice. This leaves us unable to choose our emotional responses. At the very moment we feel something painful, for example, all too often we try to evade that experience by producing an emotional reaction to it, like anger, fear, or guilt. This in turn may be too uncomfortable to experience, so we override it with some other, more acceptable response: 'I'm not angry, I'm just surprised.' Whole areas of emotion can be overrun, and we never know they've gone. Through such unconscious flinching from our experience, we can completely lose touch with the present moment.

What we think of as real emotion is often crude and superficial, expressing blockbuster feelings. This is perhaps particularly the case with men. Often we are not sure what we feel until we are overtaken by some quite strong emotional reaction; and even when we are aware of an emotional response, we are not always sure what it is. Sometimes we are too identified with our emotions to be aware of them; sometimes we deny them altogether.

There are some advantages in being able to override emotions – it can help us to get things done – but to assume on the basis of this practical ability that emotions can always be a secondary consideration is a mistake. Whether we are conscious of them or not, it is our emotions that make our decisions for us. They determine the quality of our life, the nature of our relationship to the world, and the direction in which our energy moves.

The reason we don't tend to notice emotions is because they are habitual – they are built into the world we find around us. All our experience is felt; everything we do comes, whether we know it or not, from the heart. Our emotional life is an activity rather than a passive reaction to the world. Really seeing this is profoundly liberating. I sometimes ask myself, 'Have I chosen this mental state? Where is the possibility of a little more freedom, here and now?' One could say that the Mettā Bhāvanā is the answer to these questions.

The development of universal loving-kindness

'Bhāvanā' means 'cultivation of' and 'mettā' means 'love'. This is not love as we usually understand the term. I may love my wife, my children, my friends, and my country; I may love truffle chocolates, Arsenal, Jacques Tati, and Scarlatti; but I hardly need to cultivate this kind of love, however important and estimable (or not) the objects of my partiality may be.

Mettā is different. It is impartial love – love for all living beings – and as such it is something we may not experience very often. It is emotion, but not as we know it. The experience is one of extraordinary freedom as much as anything. Mettā does not somehow obliterate our likes and dislikes, but, as we become practised at developing it, our likes and dislikes will become steadily less absolute, less rigid, less brittle. The peaks and troughs of our emotions are still there, but we become aware that they are only the surface of the ocean of our deeper connection with all that lives.

The aim of the Mettā Bhāvanā, according to the Buddha in the *Mettā Sutta*, is to develop towards all living beings the response that a mother has towards her only child. This image suggests three things. First, it is not a matter of developing a sort of lordly benevolence; it is about fashioning a living, hands-on, unbreakable bond with all other beings. In a sense it goes beyond an emotional response – it is simply the reality of the situation. Mettā is being true to ourselves and others. Second, we make mettā real not by imagining what it is like, but by bringing awareness to real emotions. And, third, mettā moves naturally towards action. The fact that a mother's activities are centred around the needs of her child gives her a very down-to-earth, businesslike attitude.

The experience of mettā is a natural, if rarely visited, extension of our most characteristically human qualities. Most of us are concerned for the welfare of people with whom we have no apparent connection. We are troubled by the sufferings of victims of oppression throughout the world, and moved when they rise up to claim their freedom. We express solidarity with others by giving to charity, donating blood, engaging in voluntary work, and so on.

So we have mettā to hand; but we may find it hard to let it in very far. Mettā loosens up our identity, and we don't want this to happen. We want to hang on to our likes and dislikes, we even want them to be absolute, incontrovertible. But the fact is that, if my circumstances were ever so slightly different, I would have a completely different set of friends, views, and attachments. I might be a Christian, or a Hindu, or a Muslim. I could so easily find myself on the other side of the fence. Indeed, a full experience of mettā leads to the realization that there isn't really a fence there at all.

Mettā is a faculty of the heart, an emotional attitude, a way of responding to living beings wherever and whenever they come to our attention. It is not speculative or abstract. But nor is it gloopy or sentimental. What others need from us is not emotionalism, but awareness and consideration. Mettā is about being able to break out of our own subjectivity and engage with another person's needs – in other words, it is a practical consideration rather than just a feeling. And this going out from ourselves produces, paradoxically, a sense of deeper integration within us. Conversely, when we cut off from others, we cut off from ourselves. This is not just theory. If you are impatient with someone, for example, you can feel this happening: something shuts down in your mind. You don't want to know.

Practising the Mettā Bhāvanā gives us a more precise awareness of other people's feelings. You find that you are able to deal more effectively with people you dislike or with whom you are upset. You aren't taken over by free-floating emotions that are not embedded in a deeper context of awareness and care, and you are better able to deal with other people's difficult emotions as well. Above all, you enjoy people more. The child in us will always enjoy being loved, but, for an adult, finding love is finding a capacity to love, to appreciate, even to relish, other people.

9

Knowing
How We Feel

*I became very interested in those thoughts of mine that I
could never catch . . . they were a dim sort of feeling.*

Ted Hughes, *Poetry in the Making*

You begin the Mettā Bhāvanā as you begin any meditation, by
bringing to mind your overall purpose and then tuning in to the
awareness in your body, preferably with some mindfulness of
breathing. Next you get a sense of the emotional texture that is
there in the breath. Or, more precisely, the emotional weather that
rolls through the breathing.

Emotions are not states of mind. They are movements of the
mind ('emote' literally means 'move out'). We may try to control
the way our emotion gets expressed but, as for the emotion itself,
this requires the more delicate touch of mindfulness. So first catch
your emotion. Big strong emotions are obviously easiest to get a
handle on. But strong emotions are generally negative ones. We
tend to give them centre stage because they give us harder ego-
definition. A creative emotion, by contrast, includes the awareness
that one's 'state' of mind is not a state but a movement. It is

therefore, in a sense, more elusive; one's energies do not gather around it so readily.

To catch the more subtle emotions that are going on all the time, you have to sit very still and quiet, like a fisherman waiting for a bite. Look out for something physical to begin with – sensations in the body, tension, or slumping – gently releasing the knots, or straightening up. You may not notice anything much at once, but you will be a bit more present, gathered. Another way into emotion is through thought: catch passing thoughts, identify them, then reel in the quality of emotion that has triggered them. Sometimes you may have to sit for quite a while waiting for a pull on the line. Or just listen for emotions until they come to your attention like the sound of soft rain on the window. Sometimes becoming aware of emotions involves separating out a muddy confusion of them. Sometimes it means knowing that you are not feeling something. Is there something you don't want to notice or think about? Without worrying about what it might be, you can just become aware of that fenced-off area in your experience.

Whether you become aware of big, uncomfortable emotions – craving, despair, jealousy, anger – or subtle evanescent ones, or nothing much at all, is not really the point. You have already started the meditation, by coming back, again and again, to being receptive to yourself.

Your positive intention in starting the practice at all is a positive emotion. Your attention to your feelings is a also a positive emotion in itself. Your posture carries an emotional tone. You can learn to recognize the emotional texture of your experience just as you recognize the colours of things.

In dealing with a problem at work, for example, there are certain emotions that help the process: inspiration, enthusiasm, humour, interest, appreciation, contentment, devotion, commitment, belief. There is no need to name them to know that they are positive – you can feel they are. They are expansive, clear, energizing, directed, flexible, and imbued with awareness. Then there are emotions that block, drain, or fragment energy: resentment, hatred, boredom, anxiety, fear, guilt, craving, cynicism. Again, you know them by how they feel. They are cold, tight, closed off, rigid, alienating, unconscious; they aren't going anywhere except round in circles.

With this awareness it is possible to learn to disentangle the complex of emotions and consciously give them a particular direction. Emotions arise, like everything else, in dependence upon conditions. If you can learn which conditions give rise to positive emotions, you can consciously set up the right conditions – at least within yourself. External conditions are not always so much within our control, of course – although some of them are.

> *My heart in hiding*
> *Stirred for a bird, – the achieve of, the mastery of*
> *the thing!*

> Gerard Manley Hopkins, 'The Windhover'

A mental state can always develop in a new direction. Confidence can be developed into faith or courage – or, if not nurtured, can degenerate into complacency. Left to itself, love may turn into clinging anxiety, and kindness may become sentimentality, but with awareness they can be developed into mettā and compassion. Once we recognize the trajectories of the heart, we can learn to set their course towards a more conscious goal.

You can't insert emotion from outside, but you can locate and nurture whatever is in there, moving in the heart, quiet seeds of feeling behind any sense that life matters absolutely; tender buds of willingness behind any belief that you can make a daily difference to your own and others' deeper happiness.

Behind a lot of people's difficulties with the Mettā Bhāvanā is I believe a misunderstanding. There is a sense that our present experience is inadequate. That we have to do something. Be different. Change our experience. So it can be very frustrating in a way that the Mindfulness of Breathing is not. But I think we underestimate the power of awareness.

Our attention, our interest by itself is enough. It is difficult to give attention, to be aware, to sit patiently, holding someone in mind, even rather distractedly, without loving-kindness being there.

Part of the problem is our identification with experience over actions. Some meditators are often I think overconcerned with triggering an emotional experience – almost anything will do so long as some kind of feeling is experienced in the practice. When the right conditions come together it can be a powerful, almost painfully intense, experience. But meditation is an activity more than an experience. It is natural to want to 'get something out of the practice'. But we are looking for something much more radical than an experience. We are looking for a different way of being with our experience, including our experience of other people. The meditation may often be uninteresting at the time, but it will have an effect. Even when there is no great feeling or emotion, my experience is that in the wake of doing the practice I find myself responding to others quite differently, and other people respond to me differently.

I remember teaching the Mettā Bhāvanā one evening many years ago, and then going out to find that my car had been towed away. It was as if I had been offered a classic opportunity to get frustrated and angry, and I just decided not to take it up. I went to the pound where it was held and paid an enormous sum of money to the poor chap sitting in a dreary little office behind thick glass, who clearly did not dare to make eye contact with his furious clients. Though it was a considerable financial blow, it was as if I had dropped all the fuss and bother of getting into a state about it, and we chatted amiably about the possibilities of appealing against the fine.

You can't force a seed to grow into a plant. All you can do – all you need do – is provide it with the right conditions. If you apply awareness, interest, persistence, and purpose, the seeds of mettā will have the light, space, soil, and wall-trellis they need. The traditional horticultural image is meant to encourage the long-term vision and patience of the gardener. Another equally relevant quality is the kind of can-do assiduity needed to get a camp-fire going on a damp evening (the Buddha talks about rubbing two sticks together). These images – both of which are useful in their own way – reflect something very important. Buddhist practice is based on conditionality: set up the right conditions and it will work. There is no spooky magic about it. If it doesn't seem to be working, cast around for anything you may have overlooked in setting up those conditions.

The main thing is not to have a fixed idea of how mettā will express itself. It is a protean faculty, emerging in all sorts of different forms depending on who or what it comes into contact with. When we see someone who is full of pain or hatred, our mettā becomes compassion; when we see someone who is full of love, mettā turns into joy and appreciation. And when we see a bird swooping and soaring, and our heart goes out to it in pleasure, that too is mettā. Mettā is a faculty that can be looked for in any situation. Ask yourself, 'Where is the mettā to be found here, now?'

10

The Mettā Bhāvanā

Who loves himself will never harm another.

The Udāna

Joy is the mother of all the virtues.

Goethe

The following version of the Mettā Bhāvanā is divided into five stages. You cultivate mettā in the first stage towards yourself; in the second, towards a good friend; in the third, towards someone about whom you feel fairly indifferent; in the fourth, towards someone you dislike; finally, you allow your mettā to spread out to encompass all human beings – indeed, all life – without exception.

Let us briefly lay out the ingredients. The practice pulls us in two directions. You are cultivating something, which means there is some future result somewhere in mind. Moreover, you are cultivating a wish, a wish that yourself and others be happy – and a wish too is inevitably for a future result.

So there is a powerful goal-orientation to the practice. But notice how, when you think of someone, you almost always have some kind of wish for them. Not consciously, perhaps, but it is there: what do you really wish for them, deep down? At the same time, a meditation is always an engagement with present experience, especially physical sensation and feeling-tone. The key to the practice is conditionality. Some obvious conditions are: you bring someone to mind; you soften, release, and straighten the posture; and you consciously, maybe verbally, wish them well. You allow these elements to work together naturally.

There are many ways to set up the conditions for the arising of mettā, and here I will suggest just a few of them. You may want to try out all the ideas mentioned, but in any given meditation session it makes sense to use just one or two of them. It would be nice to be able to say that it is 'simply' a matter of setting up conditions, but conditionality is never simple. You don't just put the nickel in the slot and get what you want. Awareness throws out all ready-made solutions. Meditation is never a repeat; it is always live. You are always addressing a different set of conditions – which of course means that you are never stuck with anything either. So can you identify a condition for the arising of mettā, at least a more positive mental state, that you could put in place now?

The first stage

So you begin with yourself. A simple way to contact mettā is just to say to yourself, 'May I be well, may I be happy.' People are often a bit sceptical of this simple and traditional strategy, but it works. Not in the way you might think, though. These plain and uncompromising words are going to awaken, I suspect – and this is the case in the other stages – a resistance to the words. When you say, 'May I be free from suffering, may I find peace', you invite a gut response: 'Well, up to a point. . .' or, even, 'I am not good enough.' Surprisingly, this can create the emotional space for mettā to be drawn out of the heart, the belly and bowels. Mettā is the basis for emotional truthfulness; so any acknowledgement of our true feelings, so long as we maintain the practice through it, takes us towards it.

You can try to see yourself as a good friend would see you, with affection. Watch yourself easing up, feel a softening around your eyes, in your jaw, shoulders, stomach. Or remind yourself of a time when you have been happy. Get back in touch with a feeling from the past – swimming lazily in the warm Mediterranean, say. Add a few details – the sky, the beach, the warmth, the lack of things to worry about – and recreate a feeling of serenity, of being composed and alive, a quiet bubbling of joy within a deep and spacious calm.

More simply, you can come back to the present and appreciate yourself at a gut level. Appreciate the miracle of sitting there being able to feel anything at all. Just enjoy having senses and look for any subtle pleasure there may be in your physical experience, any sense of poise, centredness, presence.

Or gather yourself around the heart, looking for a feeling of warmth there, perhaps a warm colour – red or gold – or a sense of opening out, like a flower. Feel the flower in your heart, its petals glowing in the light of awareness, its roots drawing on energy from below. Or, if you respond more strongly to sound than to sight, you can experience mettā as sound, as music.

It all sounds very nice, doesn't it? And sometimes it is. But this is not merely the 'feel-good bhāvanā' – and sometimes it will not feel good. The aim is to develop a sense of warmth and caring towards yourself even if – as you become aware of how you are feeling – you find that you are in some quite painful state of mind. Our problem with this practice is that a desire to be happy is often experienced as frustrated happiness, even happiness lost. It almost seems to invite in its opposite. The real problem though is that we want happiness without the frustration. The wish to be happy is really the wish to be whole. Bear in mind that meditation is open-ended. Mettā is not a mental state you get into; it is a movement, an emotional current. The active ingredient of mettā is a quality of intent. This word 'intent' is interesting because it links the idea of intensity with a sense of purpose. So mettā will often involve an intent to grow out of a comfortable state of mind into a deeper sense of your own welfare.

The second stage

In the second stage, you fuel up with the friendliness you naturally feel anyway. Think about meeting up with a good friend. It works best to choose a friend for whom your feelings are quite straightforward – or as straightforward as feelings can ever be: not someone who elicits distracting emotions like lust, regret, grief, or maternal or paternal yearnings.

See your friend in your mind's eye – perhaps imagine them approaching, and the smile on their face – then notice the response to this in your heart, the feeling of being glad at the life of another person. Or simply conjure up a sense of being with your friend: their presence, the kind of energy they generate, their rhythms of speech, the tone of their voice, their laughter. Recall a good time you had together, and look for a certain quality of response in your heart, a steady relaxation, a welling up of joy, even of celebration.

Centre your awareness around that play of emotion, that emotional gesture of reaching out to touch another person. Perhaps imagine them in a situation where they would be happy, or imagine happiness blossoming in their heart, even visualizing a flower opening there.

There are two strategies I find particularly powerful through all the stages of this practice. One is to have a sense of the person's breathing: you could make the whole practice a Mindfulness of Breathing that resonates with a sense of another's breathing. It can be the Mindfulness of Breathing with a bit of extra human interest. The other method I want to flag up here is having a sense of being seen by them. Both these methods take us right into the person's subjectivity, their inner world, while remaining anchored in our own.

The third stage

In the third stage, you allow your friend to leave and bring to mind a person you know less well, someone towards whom you are to some degree indifferent, someone you see in two-dimensional terms. Perhaps this person performs a practical function in your life, like the postman, or merely features in the landscape of your life, for instance a regular customer or fellow passenger on the journey to work.

The aim is to keep the flow of mettā going. Even though you habitually feel less interest in and concern for this person, you deliberately open up to their basic desire to be happy. You may well feel yourself zoning out of this challenge. You don't have time in your life for this person. You have nothing in common. You wouldn't know what to say to them. The aim is to acknowledge that these limitations are accidental, not essential. Just for a few minutes, put that person at the centre of your attention. Practise separating the importance of a person from their importance to you.

This stage is the hinge on which the whole meditation turns, the point at which the weight of your appreciation and warmth for your friend can swing open a gate in your heart. It is a gate we are anxious to keep closed, because we define ourselves by setting limits. Feel that resistance in your restlessness and impatience to get back to your own concerns. Imagine them breathing or imagine being seen by them. Then imagine a smile on this person's face. Imagine them in a good place. As you make space for them, imagine your heart becoming more spacious.

The fourth stage

In the fourth stage, you smuggle your mettā behind enemy lines, or rather, you smuggle your enemy into the kindly realm of your mettā. This is where the meditation starts to get a bit alchemical: in the fires of your hatred, anything soft-centred about your benevolence is burnt away, and real mettā is forged. So some genuine animosity can get the sparks flying: strong emotion is a raw material, rich in energy, if you can put it through the refinery of your attentiveness and purpose.

But to save the whole practice from going up in smoke, it may be prudent, at least to begin with, to focus on someone who merely irritates you rather than the person who has ruined your life. You may even find that someone whom ordinarily you regard as a good friend is the best bet here – and including them in your meditation may help to resolve a current difficulty. It is generally a good idea not to think or worry too much about whom to choose for any of these stages. The important thing is to sustain the flow of mettā so that you become practised in responding with kindness whenever you meet or think of anyone.

As with all the stages, keep it simple. Give yourself time to get used to your mind's tricks and tantrums. Think of meditation as a long-term thing. Relax your hands, your stomach, your hips, your shoulders, your jaw, your brows. Stay centred on your heart, and bring the 'enemy' as close as you can without letting your animosity lock in on them. Keep blowing away the storyline.

It is never comfortable to imagine how it might be to see ourselves as others see us. With this stage in particular, though, it can be interesting to get a sense of their breathing, and of being seen by them. It can wrench us out of a fixed position towards them. Suddenly you become a feature in their inner world.

The fifth stage

In this final stage, bring forward again the subjects of the first four stages – yourself, your friend, the 'neutral' person, and the 'enemy'. Search out within your heart a response that does not distinguish between them, a recognition of the beauty of life wherever and however it blooms. Allow your mettā to reach out and range over the whole world, hearing the quiet music of humanity echoing your own from every corner of the earth. The secret is in the details and the imagination. If only you observe people closely enough, try to enter their inner world, imagine their outer world, and see from where the choices they made originated, you cannot dismiss them.

Consider people of different cultures, living under all kinds of circumstances. Hear the voices of people speaking different languages. Look into their faces, into their eyes. Look out for an appreciation of all sorts of totally individual lives, balking at no one. Whether you approve of them or not, whether they are rich or poor, villains or innocents, happy or suffering, see everyone with the same eye for the irreplaceable jewel of life and the same desire for their happiness and freedom. Extend your mettā not just to human beings, but to all living things. This world is our own, it is our own life, and every living thing – every beast in every land, every bird in the air, every fish in the ocean – is real and precious. You can even go imaginatively beyond the confines of this planet, to send warmth and good will to whatever beings there may be anywhere in this universe, or any universe.

This may suggest quite a busy practice, but you will find your own way to make these connections, always remembering that the focus should be in your heart centre. At the end of the meditation come back to sitting with yourself, absorbing and dwelling in that experience of expansiveness, and preparing to take your emotional awareness and friendly intent out of their controlled environment and back into the big bad world.

11

Further Notes
on the Mettā Bhāvanā

A sentimentalist is simply one who desires to have the luxury of an emotion without paying for it.

Oscar Wilde, in conversation

He is not affected by the reality of distress touching his heart, but by the showy resemblance of it striking his imagination. He pities the plumage, but forgets the dying bird.

Thomas Paine, of Edmund Burke, in *The Rights of Man*

André Malraux, the French writer and politician, describes, at the beginning of his *Antimemoirs*, asking an old friend who has been a country priest for fifteen years what he has learnt from listening to confessions. The priest replies that he has learnt two things in the confessional: that people are much more unhappy than one imagines, and that grown-ups do not exist.

This is interesting not because it reveals that we are all sad children, but because it puts people in a completely different type of box from the one in which they usually like to appear, and the one in which we tend to put them. In the confessional we all become human and vulnerable. For some reason this vulnerability, this sense of insecurity, is something we feel we must hide. We have a strange sense that at bottom we do not really belong to the world of adults. We know that we do not understand what is going on.

I have become more and more aware over the years that most people who are introduced to the Mettā Bhāvanā do not take it up in a serious way. I think one reason is that to do it properly involves a dropping of the adult mask, the pretence that we are secure, sure of ourselves, happy in our skin.

Welcome to your world

I must lie down where all the ladders start
In the foul rag and bone shop of the heart.

W.B. Yeats, 'The circus animals' desertion'

The simile of 'inside' or 'outside' the mind is pernicious. It is derived from 'in the head' when we speak of ourselves as looking out from our heads, and of thinking as something going on 'in our head'.

Wittgenstein, lecture

It seems possible to treat the breath as a definite object of attention. Emotions, by contrast, seem more part of what we attend to things with. That is, they are part of our subjectivity. And I think what can make the Mettā Bhāvanā difficult for people is that we are chronically unprepared for the completely different way of taking things in that is involved in exploring this inner world of the mind. As an experience it is ungraspable, unreachable. As soon as you get a glimpse of some element of that subjective world it has ceased to be subjective; it has become an object. So we have to try to experience things with awareness, but without fixing them down too firmly as *objects* of awareness.

The poet Ted Hughes, in 'Myth and Education' (1976), says of this purely subjective aspect of our inner world:

> Though it is the closest thing to us – though it is indeed, us
> – we live on it as on an unexplored planet in space. It is not
> so much a place, either, as a region of events.

As Hughes goes on to explain, our inner, subjective world collides with the external, objective world at every moment. The challenge of the Mettā Bhāvanā, I believe, is to explore the contours of the inner world where it collides with the objective world. This collision between two worlds that are completely out of each other's reach is not something we normally take in.

Even the idea of an 'inner' world is in itself an avoidance of the truth of the matter. It is not – as the quote from Wittgenstein at the beginning of this section insists – literally inside us. Another poet, Stephen Spender, called his autobiography *World within World* (1951). The way he put it,

> Within each there is a world of his own soul as
> immense as the external universe and equal with that,
> dwarfing the little stretch of coherent waking which
> calls itself 'I'.

So this is a very common notion with creative writers. They are in a sense reclaiming their experience of the world. They remind us that the world is always an experience of meaning, of relationship, even when we cannot find that meaning, or we feel disconnected.

The Mettā Bhāvanā is an exploration of this world. It is a practice of attending to a world that is ours – in the sense of being our responsibility. It belongs to us. We imagine that these other people are separate from us. But they belong to us as we belong to them. Like poetry, the Mettā Bhāvanā is a redemptive process. It is about looking clearly, and this means taking an interest in everything.

Mettā is in some ways an aesthetic approach to our experience of the world. It is a sensibility that responds to all aspects of ordinary life, especially difficult, upsetting, or boring ones, with interest, humour, patience, and in the end delight. The Mettā Bhāvanā is a step up from the Mindfulness of Breathing; as does the Mindfulness of Breathing, it calls for a quality of attention to experience that is primarily interested, curious, and appreciative, rather than judgemental, calculating, and mechanical. This is relatively easy with the Mindfulness of Breathing. But with the Mettā Bhāvanā, you are taking an interest in the judgemental mind itself. It is a goal-oriented practice, so right from the start we are in judgemental mode, marking ourselves against an almost impossibly high ideal of loving-kindness for all beings. At the same time, we are deliberately calling up objects for our attention that are designed to stir up the judgemental, self-centred mind.

We all have our own way of experiencing the world, of seeing things. We all have our own inner world, populated with people, stories, and images that express for us our hopes and fears, our craving and anger, our assumptions, our judgements, our habits of mind. Of course we take this inner world very seriously. We believe in it. We are vaguely aware that others take a very different view of things from us. But, well, they are them and we are us. I saw a comedy sketch once in which two jack-booted Nazis are chatting to each other, and one of them looks ruminatively at the death's head insignia on his cap, and muses, 'Are you quite sure we are the good guys here, Hans?'

Like a lot of men, I enjoy the absurd tribal attachments of football. Nobody who cares about football pretends to be unselfish or objective in the way that people usually do. You simply don't care about the suffering of the opposition's supporters. In this, football offers a much clearer mirror to the mind than real life.

The Mettā Bhāvanā is an 'ought' or 'should' practice. You are cultivating something that you 'should' experience. In fact the Mindfulness of Breathing is also the cultivation of something – in this case concentration and clarity – it's just that it doesn't carry the same emotional load: not being concentrated does not, clearly, make you a bad person. Whereas not feeling kindness. . . ? No one wants to take in that 'I'm an unkind person' experience. But what I would suggest is that we leave being a nice person for ordinary life.

When a friend who betrays you becomes an enemy – or when you fall out of love with someone – from their end they are the same person; but in our inner world they have metamorphosed. They have taken on a different emotional identity. From being *for* us they are now *against* us. The Mettā Bhāvanā explores this unique and rich world, so bizarrely obsessed with the viewpoint and well-being of a single person, oneself. Though one's first instinct is to push all this self-centred feeling, even unacceptable feeling, out of the way, it has one or two things going for it. It has the characteristics of all aspects of the interior life in being felt, in being emotionally engaged and having meaning, even if it is a rather unedifying and unconscious meaning. It has integrity; it is real. The same goes for anything we may not like much in that interior world, for example, a negative view of ourselves, even a negative voice inside us. In the outside world all these unacceptable aspects of us need to be hidden away. Being selfish, or self-hating, is unacceptable. But as a starting point for our inner journey it's fine, it's full of interest.

In the inner world, different rules apply. As with dreams, you don't need to justify yourself, apologize, or disapprove of its contents. Or even accept them. Such attitudes should not really arise at all. Dreams and drugs give us a solitary, usually ungrounded, disconnected tour around that inner world. The artist interrogates it, bringing to the surface the profound sense of connection and integrity that belongs to it. Spiritual, religious practice connects it, by means of myth and symbol, ritual and doctrine, with the inner lives of others and with our mundane daily life.

So I think it is important to make the primary aim of this practice not to try to love everyone, or to push aside unacceptable emotions, but to be receptive to a deeper emotional reality at the core of our inner life that makes an absolute bond with the lives of others. It is a reality that can only be reached by way of the 'rag and bone shop of the heart'.

I have emphasized this inner realm in order to counteract a view we have that undermines the work of meditation. This is materialism – the view that the subjective world is not really real. It is the view that our relationship to things, the quality of our attention to things, is an inessential add-on, separable from the things themselves. It is a view that is literally soul-destroying.

I think it is important, as always, to begin and end with a sense of interest, even curiosity. What is it like to be me – or in your case, you? Of course it is difficult to say. We don't have anything with which to make a direct comparison. And of course this is itself an important element of the experience. It is incommunicable. Being 'me' is a different experience for me even day to day. So it must be utterly different for someone else. Everyone has a unique experience of being 'me'. So you take in your aloneness, the sheer particularity of this sense of being here at the centre of your world. It is an experience of particularity that no one else in your world is going to manifest. Everyone else may be compared in some way with others. But the sense of being 'me' is incomparable.

Mettā for oneself

> *Where is the mind in this tangled wood of neurons and*
> *nerve fibres? It isn't anywhere. And the self? What did you*
> *expect? A genie in a bottle?*

Paul Broks, *Into the Silent Land*

In our almost constant concern for our social identity we lose sight of the fact that the distinction between someone experienced as a self and someone experienced as another person is of a completely different order from the distinctions between people that we conventionally make.

This distinction can make the first stage of the Mettā Bhāvanā seem rather convoluted. Being friendly towards yourself, like accepting yourself, sounds nice, but in practice it can seem impossibly circular. It can be reduced to something simpler, though: the awareness of your desire to be happy. This is the key to the whole practice. If we are in touch with our own desire to be happy, that is the first thing we see in others; no living being is then alien from our sympathies.

Curiously, however, the wish to be happy can be quite hard to connect with. This is because we want a bit more than to be happy – we want to possess happiness, earn it, marry it. We are either saving it for later (being dutiful, making money, dieting, that kind of thing), or we are grabbing it now (by being greedy or lazy) and regretting it later. In these ways we slowly become indifferent to our desire to be happy. At its most extreme, the desire to be happy becomes a desire not to be who we are. It gets lost inside a desire to be rich or good or secure. The result is that we operate from a very limited identity, leaving out of consideration the larger reality of existence.

In these attitudes towards ourselves we meet the attitudes that we have towards others – kindness, indifference, hatred, lack of awareness. The Mettā Bhāvanā is incomplete without the first stage, and the first stage is developed fully only through the other stages. In our relations with others, we find out who we are. The Mettā Bhāvanā is about engaging with a larger reality out there, embodied in what we think of as 'others', penetrating the barrier that the idea of 'others' represents. We are attached to others, we dismiss others, we condemn others, we ignore others – and we do the same to ourselves because we don't see the connection.

So, as with the rest of the practice, focusing on the positive is only the beginning. The aim of the Mettā Bhāvanā is self-transformation, and we have to be careful how we think about this transformation. Buddhism makes no bones about using the language of eradication, even destruction: destruction of craving, unawareness, suffering. But this language can all too easily fuel the self-hatred that is, for many of us, at the top of the list of mental states to be 'eradicated'. Buddhism also uses the language of freeing ourselves from negative mental states but, again, this can easily turn into a kind of alienation. Mettā isn't about manipulating our emotions, or ignoring negative emotions, or persuading ourselves that we are okay. We aren't saying, 'Just for a while, may I be the kind of nice person who deserves to be happy.'

This language of destruction and freedom offers very challenging perspectives when we are ready for them. Another kind of language that Buddhism uses is that of compassion, very often embodied in the form of idealized Bodhisattvas. This language also has its danger, that of complacency, but it is probably the best language to start off with. From this perspective, real mettā has to include the stuff we don't like to look at. We may say 'May I be well,' but the caring, sharing part of us that is going to get behind that sort of sentiment is not where our real energy is kept. Before we can say 'May I be well' with the whole of ourselves, we have to identify with the whole of ourselves. Mettā for ourselves isn't just mettā for the good bits; it has to include mettā for the bits we aren't happy with – the enemy within. Developing mettā for oneself has to start with being oneself, without illusions or pretence, without excuses or blame.

All of us, from time to time, receive kindness from others. Sometimes we have a sense of beneficence from nature as well. So we don't have to think of mettā exclusively as something we try to nurture within ourselves. Instead, we can think of tuning in to it. No one 'possesses' mettā. Rather than thinking of radiating loving-kindness as though we were its source, it may be more helpful to consider that we have somehow stopped it from getting through. When we are fully ourselves, mettā is our natural response to the reality of beings. It is the most authentic response we can have. We don't put it on like a warm overcoat.

To contact mettā, you may have to pick your way through some murky areas of your experience, but, all the time, watch for a glimmer of contentment, a flicker of energy, a gap of awareness, a pinpoint of faith, a momentary lightness, a broadening, an expansiveness, a pliancy, softness, warmth, clarity of heart. Even states of mind that are seemingly unhelpful to meditation usually offer something to work with. If you are sleepy, for example, you are also relaxed, perhaps calm, peaceful, even at ease. Somewhere in that state there will be a faint glow of awareness, and you can centre on that and slowly bring the light up. Or suppose you become aware of a knot of anxiety or anger. That knot also represents an energy source that you can make use of if you can turn down the mental volume.

One tip I always find useful myself is to focus not on mettā, but on something much more specific – in the first stage perhaps gratitude, or forgiveness. Then in the second stage, perhaps non-attachment; in the third, interest; in the fourth, patience; in the fifth, openness.

Sometimes you can sit through an entire meditation session

and, in the end, have the depressing feeling that you have got nowhere at all. But the fact that you have sat down and persisted with at least the idea of mettā will have an effect, however muddy or distracted your state of mind might appear to be. Sometimes, after getting up from the cushion at the end of an apparently unproductive meditation session, one finds that – in response to meeting someone or seeing some interaction – one's heart is suddenly flooded with mettā.

Mettā for a friend

The Mettā Bhāvanā works with a basic mechanism of our emotional life. This is that whatever we give our attention to is liable to have an effect on our mental state. In turn, that state of mind influences how we see the next object. In this stage you make this whole process more conscious. You are in a sense training yourself to look out for things, for people, that nourish positive mental states. Look out for subtle pleasurable feelings in this stage.

You are also becoming aware of another natural process, that of reaching out from your own purely selfish interests, to be concerned for another person. The challenge is to be real. Ask yourself: how much happiness do you really want for your friend? How much change would you really be happy to see? A 'near enemy' of mettā is attachment, a desire for a friend to remain more or less as they are.

To develop mettā for your friend you have to let go of any claims or demands on them. You wish them well for their own sake, not yours. It is good to imagine your friend bathing in the nice warm glow that you are radiating, but it is important not to see them as somehow dependent on your radiant goodwill.

This is a good time to establish the hard-headed, unsentimental aspect of mettā. A friend is not simply someone who gives you a good feeling, but someone you look out for, and this is an important aspect of mettā that needs to be carried into the rest of the meditation: a sense that doing this meditation is going to change the way you live.

Mettā for a stranger

When we leave a friend and bump into someone we know less well, we usually find ourselves responding quite warmly to this new person. A stranger may be treated to the smile still in our eyes from our meeting with our friend. In the third stage of the Mettā Bhāvanā, you do this consciously. Not allowing the warmth to disperse, you sustain your concentration on your feeling for your friend, and in doing so you get a sense of what it would be like to care about this other, more 'neutral', person. You are not necessarily going to be taking your relationship with them beyond its present limits, but you are trying to distinguish practical limitations from emotional brick walls.

The power of good films and novels is that they introduce us to individuals we will never know, and make us care about them. They do this by focusing on the intricate interlocking of day-to-day details that on their own amount to very little, but that together add up to the kind of unique patterning we call humanity. Use your imagination to build up elements of that patterning out of whatever details you notice about this person. Their hopes, fears, and anxieties are different from ours, but we can be sure the other person has them, and that they feel as real to them as ours do to us.

With imagination we can see everyone we meet in this way. If we notice the way we look at people in the street, it is usually possible to catch ourselves making semi-conscious snap judgements: 'attractive', 'rich', 'shallow', 'scrounger'. We can dismiss someone in an instant, not seeing where they have come from or where they are going – or rather, not seeing that we have no idea where they have come from or where they are going. It is much more enjoyable and interesting to find the streets filling up with mysterious individuals. Try to allow the neutral person to be free of your projections, your habitual ways of categorizing people. Let them go their own way, be themselves, unique just as you are.

Mettā for an enemy

Hatred is a kind of attachment, and we like to have someone or something upon whom or which to vent our discomfort or pain. 'I have every right to be bitter', we cry. If we unhook that attachment, we are left with that uncomfortable feeling, even that pain, but at least that person is no longer pulling our emotional strings. Sometimes, of course, we hate someone because we have not forgiven ourselves. It may be helpful, if uncomfortable, to look for something we have not acknowledged, for which we want to be forgiven.

If you stand for anything you will sometimes have to face individuals who oppose your values. Keeping quiet, trying to be understanding, even being friendly, is not necessarily an expression of mettā, but if you are feeling mettā, you will be able to deal with people you dislike without hatred and without being false or evasive.

I think most people approach this stage wanting to retain their basic judgemental view of the person while wishing away the uncomfortable energy that it attracts. Actually we need to do the opposite – keep the interest and energy that this person stirs up while letting go of the story.

I would suggest being true to your feelings while at the same time not fixing them, not pinning them down. The way we fix our emotions is by thoughts, by judgements. 'He always does this. . . Why can't he ever. . . ?' Other people are allowed the freedom to change, to be different, complex, but we tend to lock the object of our anger into our judgement of them. Anger, hatred, is fair enough in a way – it is how we galvanize ourselves to remove a threat to our welfare. It is an essential mind function. The problem is that we turn something temporary and functional into a fixture, a final judgement. The challenge is to stay open to what is, without buying into it.

We can also actually appreciate the person we dislike. The nature of the mind is that someone has to occupy this unrewarding position in our inner life. At least from time to time. The annoying person is taking the trouble to show us round some of the less salubrious suburbs of our own mind. Through their actions and personality they give us a clearer view of ourselves. They also give us the opportunity to practise patience.

Bear in mind that the positivity you experience will be a constantly changing complex of emotions, fading out sometimes, then coming back in a slightly different mix. What you are looking for is flexibility, an ability to see beyond your limited, narrow view of the person you dislike, and break out of the mental rat run you slip into whenever their name comes up. They want what you want from life: to be happy and to be free from pain. They are going to die one day, just as you are. You can let them be more than the villain in your little drama, let them be themselves.

Universal mettā

A lot of people live on this planet, and there is a danger in this stage, if you are adept at visualizing, of churning out a kind of airline commercial, with ethnic characters from around the world waving up at you in your love-jet as you cruise at 30,000 feet. But all this should actually be taking place just under the ribs. We know we live in one world, but do we feel it? How much is it going to cost us if we do start to feel it? Look for a feeling of expansiveness, of release from a sense of reality that is centred on yourself. Surprisingly, caring about more people does not multiply one's anxieties; indeed, it tends to loosen the knots.

Mettā does not occur on its own; it comes into being in dependence on all sorts of other qualities. You aren't trying to squeeze love or friendliness out of yourself like toothpaste. You are trying to be aware of yourself and others – aware of your fear of caring too much, and also aware that your capacity to care can grow bigger. You will radiate mettā when you have set up the conditions in which it can happen. Mettā is cultivated not just by being positive and friendly but, more crucially, by being aware of that response, how it develops and how it fails to develop.

Part Four

Taking Meditation Further

12

Distractions

To be able to do one thing at a time is the whole art of life.

Sangharakshita, *Peace Is a Fire*

What isn't part of ourselves doesn't disturb us.

Hermann Hesse, *Demian*

When you start learning to meditate, it probably won't be long before you come to a conclusion that stops you in your tracks: 'I can't stop my mind wandering.' You don't have control over your thinking. As so often, the problem is actually an important insight. I know my teaching is getting through when the complaint 'I can't control my mind' is replaced by 'I've realized that I can't control my own mind. It's amazing.'

On the most superficial level, the insight is 'I am not my thoughts. I don't have to live in them or by their light.' And this is quite a liberating thought. The person I am now does not have to accept the view of things or of myself that I have inherited from the person I have been in the past.

The Buddhist view takes this idea a little deeper. I am

responsible for these thoughts: they are my mental habits – how can I pretend I am not my thoughts? But there is no separate 'I' behind my thoughts. All my thoughts and perceptions refer themselves to a non-existent source that they call the self, 'me', 'myself'.

Whatever we try to do, we are going to experience our mind. We can't magically experience another, better mind. We get distracted from the meditation because we are not content to experience who we are, the person we have chosen to be. That is, we get distracted because we are not prepared to engage with that state of mind, see it for what it is, and start turning it into a conscious activity, rather than simply an experience.

The trouble with these half-conscious thoughts and feelings drifting uncontrollably around in our mind is that they come heavily disguised. They disguise themselves as 'interesting' or 'important' thoughts, or 'yummy' thoughts, or 'quite justifiable' thoughts, or 'no thoughts at all that I could put my finger on'. So we don't see our neurotic loops of repetitive thinking as the problem. But in meditation we start to see them for what they are, as emotionally based hindrances to our welfare. And sometimes that is all we have to do to shake them off.

Here is a traditional list:

The five hindrances

- Craving for sense-objects
- Mental or physical dullness
- Hatred and ill-will
- Restlessness and anxiety
- Doubt (in the sense of an undermining scepticism) and indecision

If your emotions are more or less engaged in what you have chosen to do, you may be untroubled by this 'white noise'. In meditation, though, the white noise can turn into complete distraction. Usually, our state of mind is somewhere in between, pulled this way and that. This conflict is unhelpfully stressful and energy-draining.

These distractions represent our stock responses to life, and they constantly find events or things or people to hook onto. The same situation – the train not arriving on time, say – may provoke anxiety in me, anger in a man standing next to me, a dull weariness in a woman slumped on a bench further down the platform, a kind of escapist craving in someone beside the confectionery dispenser, and cynicism in yet another passenger reading a newspaper. The lateness of the train may seem, to each of us on the platform, to be responsible for these emotions, but they are really no more than the vehicle by which a residual emotional attitude has come to our attention. If the train had arrived on time, quite probably some other aspect of our journey would have prompted the arrival of whatever negative mental state was hovering around us.

Where do distractions come from?

Distractions are essentially unconscious; they contain no space for awareness. They seem to arise from nowhere and take over as though we had been secretly invaded. When we start meditating we have to keep them at bay while we build a bridgehead of awareness. We are then in a position to persuade them to come out slowly with their hands in the air.

Relaxed concentration inevitably brings distractions out of the woodwork, and this allows us to own them and decide what to do with them. To take a very obvious example, if we have an itch we usually scratch it automatically, but in meditation we become aware of the itch and also aware that we can choose whether to scratch it or not. The mind also has its itches. The aim of meditation is to bring every movement of the mind or body into the realm of consciousness, and thus of choice, and thus of freedom.

We are making choices all the time, mostly in an unconscious and habitual way, and experiencing the results of those choices, which are also more or less unconscious. One finds oneself opening the fridge, or picking up a book, or lighting a cigarette, or getting into a rage, or looking in a shop window, or losing heart, as one's emotional energy directs.

Meditation interrupts this process by reducing the volume of sensory objects coming to our attention. The mind continues to come up with distracting objects, but it gradually becomes obvious that at some level we have chosen them ourselves. The real obstacle to meditation (and indeed to anything else) is not that we have something to worry about, or that someone has been unkind to us, or that there is noise going on outside, or that we have an itch, or that we have something or someone very fascinating to think about, or that we can't really be sure that what we are doing isn't a waste of time. What gets in the way is that we unconsciously lose our initiative to such circumstances, and let them determine our state of mind and our whole life.

We are under the spell of the hindrances. They are pointless and sometimes painful, but they are there, unbidden. Their nature is to undermine what we are doing, whether in meditation or out of it, with conflicting thoughts, impulses, and volitions. They undermine our ability to act with integrity and wholeheartedness, but they are what they are only because they are unconscious – that is their only power. So the real work of meditation is not so much a matter of concentrating on an object as monitoring and managing the flow of mental states that emerges out of this exercise, and that either supports or undermines it.

Minding the hindrances

We want to unify our energies, and to do this we need to resolve our inner conflicts. These conflicts are 'inner' because we have to hold back parts of ourselves. (If we didn't, we would probably get ourselves locked up.) If we hold back too much, we eventually pay a heavy price. We tend to lose touch with the sources of our energy, and this results in resentment, lassitude, craving, anxiety, and doubt – yes, the hindrances.

Given that these are all expressions of conflict, you don't want to get into conflict with them. Instead, try to broaden your awareness of yourself to include other aspects as well; bring warmth and even humour into the picture. The trouble with hindrances is that they think they are the only onion in the soup and that they are going to stay that way. In fact, a hindrance is sometimes sitting on top of its opposite. Love, energy, stillness, and faith are not always comfortable states of mind, and when they are beginning to emerge, sometimes only anger, dullness, anxiety, and indecision will keep them down. So it is worth focusing particularly on whatever positive quality the hindrance may be trying to hide.

Remind yourself too that hindrances are not states of mind (as they imagine themselves to be) but movements of mind. They are moving on. If your overall mental state is fairly steady, you can just watch them pass over the sky of your mind like fluffy white clouds. That is, you encourage what is called a 'sky-like mind' or, as it is sometimes known nowadays, 'Teflon mind' or 'non-stick consciousness'.

But what if they are not so fluffy? It is useful to classify hindrances in the traditional way, usually as one of the big five, because the more generalizing we can be about them, the more easily we can distance ourselves from the personal details that draw us into them. But the reality is that they are a mix: they each depend on the support of the others. Some are simply working at much more deeply unconscious levels than others. Dullness, say, may be the most obvious characteristic of your current mental state, but you may be sure that others – frustration, resentment, craving, lack of self-belief – are in the background, producing quite an individual, personal kind of dullness that tends to come back again and again.

If, instead of experiencing occasional fluffy clouds, you experience only occasional patches of clear blue sky, you could switch metaphors and identify your regular visitors as clamouring children, each with their own tone of voice – preachy, sulky, panicky, needy, dreamy, smart-alecky, piggy, fussy, and so forth. Sometimes you may need to take control and consider what these apparently harmless children might grow into, that is, you need to take an active interest in the progeny of your own mind. It might seem as if thoughts and feelings come and go with no harm done, but a little reflection makes it obvious that they pull our strings, and we dance to their silent cacophony.

The Buddhist position is that, especially as habitual mental habits, the hindrances have a profoundly damaging effect on us. Bringing more awareness to these parts of yourself, rather than letting them run around like delinquents, will make the energy tied up in them available to you. Furthermore, if you can be an adult to your own negative mental states, you can also be an adult to the negative mental states of others. Real kindness comes not from a nice warm feeling, but from having the strength and humility to put your own feelings to one side when they get in the way.

While it is being cleared, a river will become muddy from disturbed sediment. It's the same with meditation. The process of becoming aware may make things more chaotic in the short term. Meanwhile, it is always a good idea to come back to your physical experience, relaxing and straightening your posture, in order to re-establish an essential, authentic basis of self-awareness. Hindrances can often be dealt with on the physical level. When you are distracted, come back to the straightforward authenticity of your physical experience: softening, relaxing, waking up, straightening, broadening, opening.

Sitting down with the hindrances

> *If others examined themselves attentively, as I do, they would find themselves, as I do, full of inanity and nonsense. Get rid of it I cannot without getting rid of myself.*
>
> Michel de Montaigne, *Essays*

Sometimes, a little provocatively, I say to my students, 'The reason you can't control your mind is because it is not for you to control something that is much bigger and more interesting than you are.' Your mind runs the show, and it is going to continue to demonstrate the fact until you get it. You do not pay it enough attention. You do not give it enough respect. You need to be a bit more interested in it, listen to it. If you take an interest in your distraction, your mind will stop trying to get your attention.

This is not the only misperception lying behind our attitude of frustration towards the unwillingness of the mind to play our game. We imagine that we could meditate if only we were in a different state of mind. We think that meditation can only happen on the other side of this difficulty. But we are basically looking in the wrong direction. We are turning away from something.

Now you could say that the thing to do is to 'turn towards' whatever it is. Which is a good approach, but much easier said than done. How do you turn towards the instinct to flinch away? It's like that other word for this exercise – 'acceptance'. How do you turn on something as emotionally charged as acceptance, when your experience is one of not accepting, a sense of things being unacceptable? The same goes for the invitation to be 'non-judgemental'. The instruction I prefer is, 'Take an interest.' Take another look. Sit with it a bit longer. And give yourself a break. It is difficult to be with something we would rather wasn't there. And realize that it belongs to us. It is us. Grahame Greene once said that a writer needs to have a sliver of ice in his heart. I think this is a much less evil idea than it sounds. It means writers see more and understand more because they are less reactive.

A persistent hindrance may have something to say that is worth hearing, and, if we listen, it will begin to speak to us more clearly. Our distractions sometimes carry – in their tone if not in their content – important messages. They may be the means whereby our emotions, which do not always have a direct line to our awareness, bring themselves to our attention. Alternatively, a hindrance may be our way of protecting ourselves from something. When the mind wanders off, that may be an unconscious strategy for maintaining a superficial level of awareness when we do not have the emotional resources to deal with exposure to a deeper reality.

With all the hindrances, the trick is to unhook them. It sometimes helps to think of the hindrances as creative qualities that have become entranced with the surface of our experience, like Narcissus falling in love with his own reflection, instead of looking beyond into the depths of the water below.

For example, desire can be a very positive thing – whether as a healthy appetite or as a noble aspiration. But desire can hook itself onto something and get stuck – we can't shift our desire past our craving for a cigarette, say. This is what happens to the hero of the fairy story who is given three wishes – getting stuck on limited desires, he fritters his wishes away.

It's similar with aversion. In the Greek myth of Perseus and Medusa, anyone who looks directly at the monstrous Medusa is turned to stone; but the hero Perseus approaches her by watching her reflection in his shield, then cuts off her head. Our aversion, too, gets stuck on external obstacles: a person, thing, or situation seems to bring it into being. But our enmities and hatreds must be approached as reflected images if we want to retain our freedom around them. That is, they are reflections of our own mind, of a fierce discriminating energy that we need for greater things than getting angry with others or hating ourselves.

The other hindrances can also alert us to the possibility of going deeper. If we notice that our energy is stuck in fidgeting, we can free it so that it can take us to deeper levels of concentration. As we become still, the energy of restlessness persists; it has become the pulley (the poet George Herbert's image) by which we have escaped the warm, grey fug of superficial contentment.

Similarly with anxiety. Whatever we are fretting about at the moment is almost certainly the least of what we really have to be afraid of. Anxiety hides a terror of experiencing deeper fears. As for our tendency to nod off in order to resist our experience, this can become an ability to put aside our difficulties and allow space for healing to happen in its own time and at its own level. And the fifth hindrance, doubt and indecision, can be made use of as well. If we can direct the hindrances instead of being their victim, we can learn a lot from questioning the assumptions that underlie all the hindrances, including doubt and indecision itself.

With all the hindrances we are learning a key skill at a very subtle level. The nature of a difficulty can be changed at once by a simple – though never easy – shift in attitude to it. This shift in attitude is based on a fundamental shift of view. It shifts the problem from the object (i.e. the difficulty or painful experience) to the subject (i.e. the person experiencing it). The shift is a power shift. Any difficulty, problem, or suffering is an imposition. We are subjected to it. We are pinned into our negative mental state. We get our power and our freedom back by refusing to take the negative mental state we find ourselves in as a given. Instead of being possessed by it we take ownership of it. And for this we have to take responsibility for it.

When nothing seems to work

If distractions are creating havoc in your mind, and if over time the meditation practice doesn't seem to be settling them down, you probably need to take a closer look at the conditions that have produced this state of affairs. Do you attempt to be mindful or aware outside your meditation practice? If not, perhaps the meditation on its own is not enough to deal with the backlog of unconscious impressions and reactions. Do you need to be a bit more sensitive and responsive? Are you too slack or vague? Have you taken up meditation very dutifully, so that you are keeping too tight a rein on the practice? Are you afraid something terrible will happen to you if you stop? (It won't.) Or is there some aspect of your life about which you feel uncomfortable?

You may also need to pay more attention to noticing how you feel about the meditation. Do you really want to see through your distractions, or do you, deep down, have a sense that what they are talking about is too important and interesting to dispense with?

The hindrances give us vital clues to our fundamental attitudes about what is possible for us. Do we see a clear and happy state of mind as a natural human condition that is accessible to us, or do we put limits on how clear and happy we can be? Do we think our mental state is a solid fact we're stuck with, or do we see our state of mind as essentially fluid, the product of a constantly fluctuating complex of conditions that we can change? What limits to growth do we set ourselves? Where have we put the glass ceiling? Do we take seriously the Buddhist conception of limitless potential to transform our consciousness? And, if we do, are we perhaps afraid of the responsibility that this throws on us?

Faith in meditation

> *Who would have thought my shrivelled heart*
> *Could have recovered greenness? It was gone*
> *Quite underground; as flowers depart*
> *To see their mother root, when they have blown.*

George Herbert, 'The Flower'

We think of being able to concentrate as an ability to apply ourselves to something dull. Actually it is an ability to find things – to find life – rich, complex, and deeply satisfying. We say, 'My mind wanders', but what that means is that only part of the mind is engaging itself – and rather a small, shrivelled part at that. Meditation is subject to the same habits that govern the rest of our lives: we may end up doing it because we are afraid of the consequences of not doing it, or because we want approval, or because it's our job, or because we have always done it, or because we hope to get something for nothing from it.

With the Mettā Bhāvanā as well, it is worth reminding yourself that you are wishing people well not because you necessarily feel anything particular towards them. You wish them well out of a faith that mettā is your true nature, even if you are not in touch with it at the moment.

When you first learn to meditate, the practice has its own significance. It is something you do for its own sake. Later on, you might do it in the same way you snatch breakfast in the morning. It's a utilitarian thing, a means to an end. This is natural enough. You're busy. But eventually you have to find again that beginner's attitude to meditation. It isn't just something you get out of the way so that you can get on with what is more important. It's like having a good dinner: you need its energy in order to do other things, but enjoying the food for its own sake may also help you to digest it properly.

Because it is something you do on your own, it is easy to forget that the significance of meditation lies not only in its effect upon you. Whether implicitly or explicitly, you are meditating for the sake of others, and it helps to remind yourself of the wider patterns created by your efforts and intentions. A simple way to do this is to try a devotional practice. Staying in touch with the significance of meditation will help you through the times when you don't seem to be benefiting from it. Sometimes you just have to nourish the roots, keep coming back to the practice, and wait for spring to arrive.

13

Balanced Effort

You can't beat hens to make them lay.

Marianne Moore, 'The Student'

It isn't possible to have a meditation practice without the discipline to work at it regularly, whether you feel like it or not. The idea of any practice, whether it's musical, artistic, sporting, intellectual, or meditative, is to impose something on yourself, and demand something of yourself, not for money or fun, but for the joy and the love of it. Meditation gives you the momentum to take you through your present difficulties, and, when it is going well, a commitment develops that will see you through. However, when the going gets tough, you will often find that trying harder doesn't work. When meditation seems really hard, even painful, you may knit your brows, clench your brain, and try to accelerate past all the unnecessary feelings and mental processes that get in the way of what you think the experience should be like, but somehow you get no closer to that experience.

On the other hand, not making an effort doesn't seem to work either. If you don't make any effort, you drift and become vague about what exactly you are doing. In the end you don't really see the point of meditating at all.

To begin with, it can be a huge effort just to sit still for ten minutes and keep returning your attention to the focus of the meditation. But you have to relax that effort each time before you try again. It's like learning to drive a car. To get into gear you need to push down the clutch pedal, but to get going you need to release it again: the process is an engagement followed by a letting go. This becomes a smooth manoeuvre when you're used to it, but, while you're still learning, the car is going to judder and jerk. Similarly, although depth in meditation comes through engaging more and more of your energy, this is not achieved by making more and more effort. Effort is necessary at first, but the next step is to reduce the effort.

What you're aiming for is a bit of a stretch, without being grabby. Less is more – and more difficult. You need to make just enough effort to enable you to attend to what is going on at this moment. Any more means that you are reaching out to experience something else; and if you do that, you will miss the present moment altogether. The harder you concentrate, the less you are aware. We want results, and if possible a shortcut to those results. Ideally we'd like to make the effort, get the results, and relax. But the kind of effort you need is the kind of effort required to listen to your child when you have a hundred and one things to do by last Tuesday. However important the things on your to-do list are, it is almost always more important to listen to that message from the present, trivial as it may seem.

Effort in meditation is not 'an' effort. There is no point at which you stop making it. It is as little effort as is required, sustained as fully you can manage. It is a continuity of effort – that is, it has to be combined with mindfulness. It's like covering a statue in gold leaf. The whole thing has to be covered, but too thick a covering will destroy its definition. At no point on the surface will you find more than the finest layer of gold – yet the effect is to transform the image. The result of this balancing of gentle effort with mindfulness is perseverance.

I present this key element in meditation in this way because, for many people, making more effort is the easy option. It requires no imagination or awareness. Balanced effort is effort balanced with other qualities, and it has to be kept in the background to allow the shyer qualities through. In judo – to take a classic example – it may seem as if all you need do is make a bit more effort, and your opponent will fall over. If he is small enough this may well happen, but, in the long run, making more effort is going to get in the way of learning how to put down even the strongest opponents – getting your grip right, breaking their balance, timing, stepping, turning, pulling, and so on. Once everything is in place, you can bring to bear against the big guy a huge effort that is not willed effort, not just a call for exertion from 'head office', but rooted effort, effort that is embodied, that explodes from the earth, through the toes, right up to the fingertips.

The Buddha likened balanced effort to tuning a stringed instrument. The strings, he said, should be neither too slack nor too tight. Another way of putting this is to say that the right kind of effort has been achieved when the whole body of the instrument vibrates. Indeed, one of the great judo champions of recent years, Robert van de Walle, who was well known for the powerful physicality of his judo, enjoyed a notable come-back late in his career, after his English trainer made him sing as part of his training.

If your practice is lazy, dull, and uninspired, more effort alone won't work. Meditation engages us in something that runs counter to our normal interests. For it to be effective, we have to leave behind our desire for sense experience, and to do that we have to feel a real dissatisfaction with that ordinary mental state together with a real interest in developing something else. The only way to do this is to believe that there is something else. Whether you were aware of it or not, this faith got you meditating in the first place; you might as well continue to use it. Instead of pushing yourself to meditate, find something to pull you. If you bring faith in the possibility of change into contact with your perseverance, you will develop an unshakeable determination that will take you as far as you want. To begin with, you will have to keep hauling your attention out of a rut, but after a while your concentration will be rolling and you'll just have to keep the towing rope taut.

Once your concentration is established, you can move in on the object of your meditation, make closer contact with it, look for a clearer definition. Then relax, loosen up, broaden the field of your awareness. If you become distracted or a bit dull and woolly, focus on the object again. Gradually, as your energy becomes more concentrated, this adjustment will become more subtle. The aim is a steady accumulation of energy, gradually bringing all your resources to bear upon the object, while maintaining your awareness.

Outside meditation you may need to put in rather more effort to remain aware, because you will have rather more than your own mental states to be aware of. One starts meditation thinking it will sort out one's head. What one finds, however, is that this involves sorting out the heart as well, and that this means moving on from oneself to become more aware of others. And people can be more work (as well as fun) in the flesh than in the freeze-frame of meditation. There is a whole genre of stories about monks or hermits emerging into the world after years of meditation and proceeding to make complete asses of themselves.

14

Concentration

That blessed mood . . .
In which the burthen of the mystery,
In which the heavy and the weary weight
Of all this unintelligible world,
Is lightened: – that serene and blessed mood,
In which the affections gently lead us on, –
Until, the breath of this corporeal frame
And even the motion of our human blood
Almost suspended, we are laid asleep
In body, and become a living soul:
While with an eye made quiet by the power
Of harmony, and the deep power of joy,
We see into the life of things.

Wordsworth, 'Tintern Abbey'

I may not hope from outward forms to win
The passion and the life, whose fountains are within.

S.T. Coleridge, 'Dejection: An Ode'

There are all kinds of situations in which we need to concentrate, but we usually get concentrated by excluding parts of ourselves from our awareness – often our body and our emotions – in order to complete the task in hand. In this way our energies are divided – parts of us are elsewhere, making themselves known only in the form of hindrances – and we experience more or less unconscious conflict. In meditation, however, we welcome these conflicting parts of ourselves into our awareness, with the result that we eventually become truly concentrated and harmonized. This harmonized condition of being is self-created. We are no longer trying to wring satisfaction out of the world by plugging into sense experience; we have our own generator. The result of this is that we experience great joy.

As you sit to meditate, look for the joy that comes from being very clear about, and intensely interested in, what you are doing. You may notice resistance to this, a subtle sense of withdrawal and disconnection, or a sense of grabbiness or overshooting. This is distraction working at a more refined level. Engaging in a process that takes us beyond the orbit of the small self with its anxieties and vanities, we have a natural fear of releasing too much energy and an equally natural desire to appropriate the whole experience.

If you manage to sustain a sense of contentment and enthusiasm, at some point you will notice that you have left behind any sense of distraction or resistance. You begin to experience the natural results of being happy, fulfilled, and content, free from inner conflict. You still have to keep setting up the conditions for a deeper concentration. You continue to give your attention to what is present before you rather than what you would like to be there. But you become very still. It is as if the stillness soaks through your body and mind until your whole being brims with quietness. As that peace spills over into pleasure, you may get a bit grabby or fearful, and the concentration may slip away. When this happens, you can just smile and make another approach.

Sooner or later you may find yourself suffused with a tangible yet subtle physical pleasure, an intense comfort and clarity of body and mind. As you maintain a delicate but totally continuous contact with the object of concentration, this focus will be haloed by a warm and clear awareness of thoughts and feelings. Any emotional knots you encounter will no longer have the power to distract you. Your thoughts will be pliant and responsive, and you will be able to direct them without arousing resistance, distraction, or dullness. Your reflections will have an emotional warmth to them, and a brightness, as if they come mounted on velvet. Or you will become like an eagle – totally focused, watchful, but at the same time floating pleasurably on upward currents of emotional warmth.

This state of mind is the first stage of concentration, the first of four dhyānas, as they are called. It can be a surprise at first that such a state of mind is freely available, once you can contain your emotional energy instead of being stuck in it. But once you have experienced dhyāna, you begin to become more sensitive – in everyday life as well as in meditation – to how you can cultivate this freeing up of your mental states. A crucial factor in the development of meditative concentration is pleasure. The quality of the positive feeling develops and becomes more refined as the concentration deepens, but it is always there: concentration and pleasure, even bliss, arise in dependence upon each other.

In the second dhyāna, you are filled with delight and rapture, and experience a tremendous movement of energy in the subtle experience of your body, particularly as emotional blocks are released. You may no longer need the support of the meditation technique; you just keep directing attention towards certain qualities or tendencies in your experience, especially attending to any feelings of pleasure in your body.

Gradually you become so absorbed in, even transported by, that welling up of rapture – experiences of tingling and intense but subtle vibration – that you stop reflecting upon your experience. You are aware of what is happening, but your experience is not on an everyday, conceptual level; it is more visionary. You may not literally experience visions, heavenly music, or divine messages, but this is the level on which such experiences can occur. You may experience temperature changes and, more typically, your body may shake and shiver. The aim is to contain this energy, and to sit as still as possible without actually suppressing the energy.

With the arising of the third dhyāna, having allowed rapture to fill you and having experienced the bliss of that fulfilment, you feel the rapture fade away to leave a deeper, more purely mental bliss. It is as if that bliss is hidden in the rapture, just as the rapture was hidden in the concentration of the first dhyāna, and as all the joys of the dhyānas are hidden in the messy everyday mind. This is simply to say that we all have this hidden potential, and that it is the business of meditation to uncover it. In the third dhyāna you experience scarcely any separation from the rest of life. Integrated within, you are connected to a greater reality.

As absorption deepens further, the feeling becomes more and more refined until you are absolutely still. This is the fourth dhyāna, and it takes one outside the categories through which one usually experiences the world (like 'mind' and 'matter'). It is therefore from this ultimate state of human integration that supernormal powers develop.

The higher dhyānas (and there are more even beyond the fourth dhyāna) represent very rarefied states of consciousness indeed. But the first dhyāna is within easy reach; in fact, you don't have to be sitting in meditation to experience it. Even the second dhyāna is sometimes experienced – particularly in connection with the fine arts – by people who have never concerned themselves with meditation as such. By the same token, you can support the arising of dhyāna wherever you can bring a limpid intimacy of attention to things, the kind of subtle vibrancy of perception that is perhaps more easily accessed in our response to music, art, and so on.

Meditative concentration is a concentration of energy. This is not always comfortable. It can be very uncomfortable. Energies in the body can seem to develop a life of their own, that the body can hardly control. One may be visited by coloured lights of one kind or another, or intense lucid dreams. One may get flashes of what others are thinking, or even strange predictive moments, where one knows what is going to happen before it does.

Interesting as these events may seem in the abstract, what is disturbing about them is the sense of loss of control. And they can be quite exhausting. The way to work with these events is really no different from working with any difficult mental states. The part of you that is able to react with panic or despair comes from the part of you that is also able to step back and contain the experience. As always with mindfulness, you take in the whole of your experience, grounding the troubling material in an awareness that includes more humdrum aspects of your experience. You also take in your experience as something impermanent, changing. And, finally, you only have to deal with anything in the moment.

15

Taking in the View

'All things whatsoever are devoid of unchanging selfhood.'
When one sees this with insight one becomes weary of
suffering. This is the Way to Purity.

The Buddha, *Dhammapada* XX 7

People who take up meditation tend to pride themselves on being open-minded. It is considered a good thing not to hold firm clear views, not to take a definite stance. It is considered presumptuous to firmly disagree with others. People are perhaps quite reasonably anxious about being one-sided.

I'm afraid I'm not sure about this. It is true that one of the ways in which the goal of Buddhism expresses itself is in a freedom from views. But what this means is that the Enlightened person is not emotionally attached to their views. He or she will still be quite clear about their views.

One of the most original contributions of the Buddha to human knowledge is his discovery that theories are rooted in desires. Our views are never objective. This is well known nowadays. Many of the views we consciously hold have their unconscious roots in our feelings.

I hope I have shown a few instances of how our meditation practice can be at the mercy of quite basic assumptions of how things are. Ideas about what you are capable of, what meditation can do for you, what the nature of your experience is, what is true. You can work hard at your practice for years without realizing that you hold a basic view that renders the whole exercise fairly superficial.

Every moment we are telling a story: of ourselves, of others, of the world, of the nature of reality. We are making sense of our experience. These stories are largely unconscious assumptions about what is going on, a whole set of interpretations and judgements of our experience that lie behind the way we act, speak, and think. Unquestioned attitudes lie deep in our conditioning. We are the way we are because of the meaning we give to our experience of this moment. This is not essentially an intellectually worked-out view, but an emotional, unconscious, habit of mind.

We can't not have a view

Our views are built into the fabric of our life. They are the way we experience things. Becoming more conscious of them helps us to pin down and challenge some basic tendencies towards certain negative emotional reactions that are based in them. At the same time we should be clear that we are not going to change our views just like that. We may want to change them on an intellectual level, but at an emotional level changing them would oblige us to change the way we live. So one has to be realistic.

It is said that when the Buddha was teaching he was sometimes accompanied by a mythical protector figure called Vajrapāṇi, who would appear when someone was refusing to answer a question put to them by the Buddha. Vajrapāṇi carries a vajra or thunderbolt (like the Greek god Zeus) and he would threaten to split the stubborn person's head if they continued to refuse to answer. So he was known as the protector of the truth. Life is always interrogating our basic take on life. By refusing to take in the mismatch between what our immediate experience is telling us and what our views insist is the case, we produce a chronic internal split. Nietzsche famously and sardonically observed:

'I have done that' says my memory; 'I cannot have done that' says my pride; eventually, memory yields.

Views of ourselves

Some of our views are psychological. We develop a fixed view of ourselves that is very much based on others' view of us. In general we tend to allow other people to judge us and thus we maybe look for others' approval or sometimes, of course, their disapproval. Here are just a few unhelpful views of ourselves to look out for:

- I am a failure. Things that might work for others will not work for me.
- Things have a natural tendency to go wrong.
- I am essentially unlovable, worthless.
- I must cover up what I really am with something much more acceptable.
- I can reasonably expect other people to be reasonable. It is reasonable for me to get angry. It is unreasonable for other people to get angry.
- I am special; therefore other people should do what I wish and should not have what I don't have.
- I shouldn't have to experience unpleasant feelings.

Views of life

Some of our views are more existential. They concern the basic dynamics of existence, the very nature of how life works. Here are a few unhelpful ones to look out for:

- I have to have some other experience from this one in order to be happy.
- If I stop worrying something will go terribly wrong.
- This moment has to serve some purpose beyond itself; I have to become better. I and everyone else have to justify our existence. In fact, everything must be instrumental to something else. Everything is a means to an end, not an end in itself.
- Falling short of the ideal is not good enough. If nothing terrible is happening it is still not good enough. If I have a reasonably functioning human body that is not enough. The experience of this moment must be somehow special.
- This tiny step I take in the direction of being more aware is useless.
- If I have problems something is going wrong.
- It is reasonable to expect things to be permanent and perfect.
- This state of mind now is of absolute importance.

You may wonder why I advise looking out for negative views. Why not look out for positive ones? I think the key issue here is being true, seeing the truth of one's actual view. That is where real change happens. The temptation is to plaster the positive view over the top of the real one. As so often, we have a natural tendency to favour control over awareness.

Views of reality

Our deepest and most unconscious views are about how things really are and who we really are:

- Do you regard the narrative you are playing out, which forms your identity, as absolutely real?
- Do you regard the world as you experience it as the absolute reality of the world?
- Do you believe that the way you see yourself is the way you actually are?
- Do you think that being aware, your sense of being here, originates in your head, your thinking?
- Do you think awareness is a feature of the self? Or is the self a feature of awareness?
- Do you regard your state of mind as your own affair, or does it affect others?

Maintaining views

We may not acknowledge our views consciously. But emotionally and instinctively we hold onto them. We construct our sense of ourselves out of them.

So we have a story, particularly about ourselves. But then something happens that doesn't fit with the story. So what do we do with this experience? We will tend to make it fit with our view or story anyway. So the view is constantly maintained by a limited pattern of thinking, a way of framing or filtering any experience in the same way.

Working with views

I think it is important to be able to hold definite and firm views about things, while remaining open to being persuaded otherwise. We need to take a definite stance, and to look for reflections of our basic views in the way we behave, the way we react emotionally, our habits of mind.

Coming back to our actual experience here and now, we can begin to catch sight of a reality that is not framed by old, narrow, and sometimes even toxic patterns of thinking. We can start to loosen the hold of unconscious views on the way we experience ourselves and the world. We can develop clearer views. In the end, the Buddhist goal is to become free of views altogether. 'When the answers are in your being', as my teacher Sangharakshita puts it, 'you have no need to keep them in your head.'

16

Insight Meditation

Meanwhile the mind, from pleasure less,
Withdraws into its happiness; –
The mind, that ocean where each kind
Does straight its own resemblance find; –
Yet it creates, transcending these,
Far other worlds, and other seas;
Annihilating all that's made
To a green thought in a green shade.

Andrew Marvell, 'The Garden'

If you do not expect the unexpected, you will never find it.

Heraclitus

Meditation is a means of developing our natural capacity for joy and love. But how far can we take it? On what does this capacity of ours depend? What happens when our world falls apart, when people close to us die when they aren't supposed to, when we grow old or helpless before we're ready? Underneath our joy and love, what waits for us? What do we do with the aspects of our experience that are not touched by joy and love: fear, grief, rage, and humiliation? The refined, positive states of mind we develop in meditation are not ends in themselves. Our new-found serenity must be tempered by a meeting with the real facts of life.

These facts are what we are most afraid of, and our lives are built around their avoidance, but according to Buddhism we suffer not because we cannot avoid them but because our whole being is committed to trying to avoid them – trying to avoid aspects of life that, ultimately, are unavoidable. In the end, we are not in control. Buddhism is basically concerned, through the practice of ethics and meditation, with loosening up the self-protective habits of the mind, the wonderful evolutionary adaptations we have all inherited from millions of years of trying to control our environment. The idea is to allow something to emerge, or to awaken, that is not part of that mechanism for controlling our experience that we call the self. This something is called vipassanā, or insight, even transcendental insight – 'transcendental' because it transcends one's previously limited perspective. It is the awakening mind, or big mind. When it emerges, we are no longer totally identified with the self or terrified of its inevitable demise, and we are free from having to cater to its impossible demands. A burden is dropped.

This sounds great, but anyone who has had a glimpse of awakening before they are ready will testify that it is also unbearable. And in some sense the converse applies: what is unbearable is of the same nature as awakening.

Insight is the nature of reality coming right down to earth and breaking in upon our cosy delusion. The nature of reality makes an appearance in any experience of failure, loss, or humiliation. It is there whenever our sense of ourselves cracks open, whenever we feel exposed, wronged, or grief-stricken. A cherished plan fails, a lover walks out, a letter brings terrible news, and the cold shock of reality shakes us, for a while, into being more real. And

118

– perhaps this is even harder for us to take – sometimes beauty, joy, or love shakes us to the core too; it can pierce us to the heart in a way that is almost physically painful. One can also say that there is an element of insight in the strange sense of liberation and happiness that sometimes arises within a context of painful loss. As the travel writer Freya Stark writes in her autobiography, 'The beckoning counts, and not the clicking of a latch behind you.'

When someone who is part of our life dies, we have the sense of some deep root being broken, and this experience is the closest most of us come to real insight. Witnessing a death, we experience the nuts and bolts of being human. Death is very ordinary. It is a humdrum business with all sorts of practical details to be attended to. The clocks don't stop – life goes on. And in some sense insight involves the coming together of these two things – ordinary life and ordinary death – because it is fundamental to our delusion that we leave death out of our experience of life.

In fact, insights call out to us every day, but we don't usually hear them because they challenge us, they reverberate with implications for how we should live. An insight is essentially a recognition, an acknowledgement of some truth. It stops being an insight when we find a way of separating that recognition from how we go about our life. To take a simple example, we may see very clearly that there is no justification for the existence of industrial abattoirs just to provide us with our taste pleasures, but we cannot resist that bacon sandwich, because understanding is not the same as insight. Likewise, the experience of someone close to us dying only turns into an insight to the extent that it changes the way we live. The insight or realization may not come to us at the time. It is more likely to dawn later. Like Wordsworth's definition of poetry, it arises from 'emotion recollected in tranquillity'.

Meditation as a process of integration is important to insight because it interrupts our normal way of processing our experience. The way we usually learn is by adding more and more material, as if the mind were an enormous filing cabinet. Being able to compartmentalize our experience in this way is a useful accomplishment: it enables us to do things half-consciously, and so allows us to do things we don't feel like doing, but it does make it difficult for a complete shift in our being to take place. One reason books that promise to 'change your life' don't generally do so is that our unconscious response is to open a new file labelled 'life-changing experiences'.

Buddhist meditation gradually replaces this filing cabinet with a living relationship to our experience. 'Having experiences' becomes a constant reconfiguring of the relationship between the self and the world. If our attitude is one of consuming experience, there is only going to be room for our experience to come to us in the form of a verbal report for immediate filing. The only way truly to experience anything is to be changed by it – or rather, in it. To experience mettā or compassion is to listen to what it says about our way of living.

We originally overcame our fear of the world by knowing it and naming it, but through this knowing we now hold the world at arm's length. By knowing our way around the world, by knowing exactly what is going on, we allay our anxiety, but we also feed it, because underneath there is a growing uneasiness at our ignorance about what is really going on. In meditation we start unknowing things – that is, we make our experience conscious rather than unconsciously filing it away – and begin to gain access to a deeper knowledge.

The Mettā Bhāvanā and the Mindfulness of Breathing prepare us for insight to arise by quietly and steadily undermining fixed ideas and rigid emotional attitudes, so that we may sustain and accept the ultimate deconstruction of our experience of reality rather than being overwhelmed by it. Any meditation can bring home to us certain radical insights, and even, if we add a reflective element to it, contain the possibility of transcendental insight. Impermanence can be realized by just watching the breath come and go.

However, there is a particular class of Buddhist meditation, called insight meditation, which is specifically concerned with the contemplation or interrogation of reality. It comes in all sorts of forms, some simple, some weird and wonderful. The general principle is that one contemplates something – whether cognitive, perceptual, or symbolic – designed to trigger insight. You can contemplate reality in the form of a symbolic visual image together with a mantra. You can turn over in your mind a Zen kōan, a type of question to which there can be no rational reply. Or you can minutely examine your sensations, feelings, and mental states, and observe how they arise in dependence upon one another, and how none of them has any independent or permanent existence.

The practice of insight begins with unremitting reflections on the most fundamental existential questions. These reflections are sustained until they gradually begin to colour or flavour one's whole experience of life. Then, in meditation, one contemplates this developing sense of the way things are, bringing to that contemplation all the qualities one has developed through one's meditation practice: a fully integrated mind, steady, expansive, and untroubled by any discomfort of mind or body.

All this prepares us for insight – but we can't summon it up deliberately. The term 'Buddha' means 'one who is awake' – but the dreaming mind can only dream; it is the awakening mind that awakens. In the end, we will awaken to reality not by telling ourselves what is real, or how reality works, but by being more real. Beyond having ideas about reality – in a scientific, philosophical, or religious sense – we must prepare to meet it at every moment, both in meditation and out of it. We prepare to meet it by the constancy and kindness of our attentiveness, not allowing any part of our life to hide away from our meditation practice, and not allowing our practice to ring-fence any other part of our life.

We prepare the ground by reminding ourselves that we are dreaming, and by being a bit clearer and more aware about the way we ordinarily see things. Contemplating reality is about bringing our thinking home, to the heart. As well as trying to be more continually attentive, we greet everything that comes to our attention as an introduction to some aspect of reality. For example, non-dual experience is an essential basis for insight, but one doesn't get there by imagining non-duality. One prepares for it by taking in more carefully the straightforward duality of one's way of looking at things, by becoming aware of the lines one is always unconsciously drawing between oneself (or the various groups of family or tribe with which one identifies) and the world that lies outside that constantly shifting magic circle.

We may try to reflect upon how things decay and die, we may try to observe how we ourselves decay and die, but observing ourselves in this way still leaves the self triumphantly secure, observing. To contemplate impermanence itself is really impossible. All we can do is contemplate ourselves as we try futilely to create permanence out of houses, jobs, relationships, and all the rest of it. By patiently stripping away our repeated attempts to cover up the indecent fact of our own mortality with a blanket of abstractions, we steadily begin to corner reality even before we get a glimpse of it.

What we contemplate in this kind of meditation is how we go about experiencing and responding to things. Contemplating reality sounds very grand, but it is just a matter of becoming clearer about what we think of as ordinary reality. One may contemplate conditionality – that is, how things arise in dependence upon conditions, how nothing exists in isolation – but the point of this practice is not to get a theoretical understanding of this process, but to find it taking place in ourselves, here and now, unravelling everything upon which the mind tries to fix itself.

When we are on our own, with nothing to do, we naturally

give ourselves up to daydreams and distractions. But there is something more interesting we can do. We can turn things over in our minds, question the assumptions and concepts that guide the way we live. What do we really believe in? What do we put our heart into? Where do we find our joy? In this way, we turn over the mind as a gardener works the earth, breaking up the ground to make it more fertile.

The teachings of Buddhism exist less to provide answers than to provide the tools and the light by which we may investigate ourselves at ever deeper levels. Thus meditative concentration takes our reflections further by refining our conceptualizations. To take a simple example, in the Mettā Bhāvanā, you may start by verbalizing – 'May she be well' – but the words should gradually soften until eventually you are in some sense saying the words without them crossing your consciousness at all. In the same sort of way, the breakthrough to insight comes when your thinking has become so subtle and refined that understanding shifts subtly into insight, like the shift from thinking about something to simply seeing it. It is analogous to how, when you become really concentrated on your breath, your consciousness of the breath itself seems to disappear.

The essential prerequisite for insight practice is concentration. I would also add pleasure and happiness. You won't be able to take in the nature of reality unless you feel basically okay with yourself and the world. It is said that trying to develop insight without concentration is like trying to keep a candle alight in a draughty room. Cognitive activity in dhyāna is more refined than our everyday mind – more penetrating, intuitive, positive, flexible, and aware – and these qualities are intensified if they are imbued with the flavour of the experience of the higher dhyānas. But the higher dhyānas are not where insight actually takes place; insight meditation is practised most effectively at the level of the first dhyāna, where we are still connected to our ordinary experience through conceptual thinking (which is not present in the higher dhyānas), or in 'access concentration', the concentrated state that precedes the arising of the first dhyāna. The quality of attention we develop in concentrated meditation, and particularly in the Mettā Bhāvanā, is the kind of open, receptive, positive, even playful, interested focus that we need in order to really see the mind and body operating without our familiar interpretations blanketing them over. The fact that your experience feels elusive and difficult to grasp is fine – you are getting a bit of insight into its true nature. A sense of disorientation and frustration is part of the process. What this does mean though is that we need a lot of determination, faith, and support in order to push through long periods of meditation practice.

The Buddha's original problem was that, however deeply he experienced his own nature in meditation, when he emerged from those heavenly realms of dhyāna he found that the reality of his nature could not be separated from the reality of others, that it was constructed in the world outside the matrix of his meditation practice. He discovered that reality could not be found within the separate experience of the self, however refined or godlike this might be. In order to gain insight, the fully integrated mind has to surrender that divine self-sufficiency. The Buddha designed his mindfulness practice specifically so that the concentrated mind could establish a critical engagement with the world that would unpick the fabric of its delusion and suffering.

The other major prerequisite for insight is faith: to wait without any expectation or hope – for hope, as T.S. Eliot says, would be hope for the wrong thing – in the confidence that insight will reveal itself to us, like watching for a rare bird to dart before us. If we have decided to contemplate a Buddhist doctrine like the four noble truths, for example, we stop trying to understand them, and just deepen our receptivity to them. Reality is not to be understood according to any categories, and as we habitually understand things by categorization, this leaves us unable to take any steps towards it, or even to invite it. Instead, we can become aware of an ever-increasing build-up of pressure as our gradually clarifying perspective on reality bears down on our deep but ever more vulnerable emotional investment in the way we usually see things.

> That scrawny cry – it was
> A chorister whose C preceded the choir.
> It was part of the colossal sun,
> Surrounded by its choral rings,
> Still far away. It was like
> A new knowledge of reality.

> Wallace Stevens, 'Not ideas about
> the thing but the thing itself'

The arising of transcendental insight is not like having an idea or even an ordinary insight. It seems to come not from inside oneself but from outside. It is not something that one's own mind comes up with. It is not a concept or even an emotion, nor is it necessarily a blinding flash, or a road-to-Damascus experience. Visionary experience may contain an element of insight, or it may not. A deep sense of faith, joy, even fear may have the perfume of transcendental insight, or it may not. This insight is perhaps most likely to emerge simply as a subtle yet powerful sense of some fundamental and inexplicable shift in one's being.

We protect ourselves, and our sense of our own centrality, by reading the world rather than living it, by clinging to the idea of the thing rather than experiencing the thing itself. Actually to see another person is a tremendous threat to our own centrality. To go out to meet the world and engage with it directly rather than through the mediation of our ideas, our prejudices, our religion, leaves us with nothing really secure. But this is the open heart of Buddhist meditation.

Meditation Postures

One leg in front

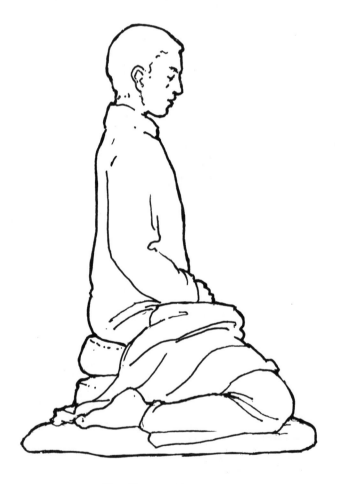

Kneeling astride cushions

Recommended Reading

Ayya Khema, *Being Nobody, Going Nowhere*, Wisdom Publications, Somerville, MA 1987. Few good writers on Buddhism have this German Theravādin nun's depth of spiritual experience.

Kamalashila, *Buddhist Meditation: Tranquillity, Imagination and Insight*, Windhorse Publications, Cambridge 2012. A clear and comprehensive guide to Buddhist meditation.

Macy, Joanna, *Mutual Causality in Buddhism and General Systems Theory*, State University of New York Press, Albany, NY 1991. A brilliant illumination of the fundamental principle of Buddhist thought.

Ñāṇamoli, *The Life of the Buddha*, Buddhist Publication Society, Kandy 1992. A classic collection of translations from the Pali suttas.

Paramananda, *Change Your Mind*, Windhorse Publications, Cambridge 2010. A warm, human, and accessible basic introduction to meditation.

—, *A Deeper Beauty*, Windhorse Publications, Birmingham 2001. An assortment of inspiring reflections and exercises around everyday practice.

Sangharakshita, *Who Is the Buddha?* Windhorse Publications, Cambridge 2012.

—, *What Is the Dharma?* Windhorse Publications, Cambridge 2011. More from the author's own teacher.

Meditating

Shunryu Suzuki, *Zen Mind, Beginner's Mind*, Weatherhill, New York 1999. Profound teachings on Sōtō Zen meditation.

Sogyal Rimpoche, *The Tibetan Book of Living and Dying*, Rider, London 1998. A beautiful and imaginative summation of a great teacher's understanding of the Tibetan approach to death.

WINDHORSE PUBLICATIONS

Windhorse Publications is a Buddhist charitable company based in the UK. We place great emphasis on producing books of high quality that are accessible and relevant to those interested in Buddhism at whatever level. We are the main publisher of the works of Sangharakshita, the founder of the Triratna Buddhist Order and Community. Our books draw on the whole range of the Buddhist tradition, including translations of traditional texts, commentaries, books that make links with contemporary culture and ways of life, biographies of Buddhists, and works on meditation.

As a not-for-profit enterprise, we ensure that all surplus income is invested in new books and improved production methods, to better communicate Buddhism in the 21st Century. We welcome donations to help us continue our work - to find out more, go to www.windhorsepublications.com.

The Windhorse is a mythical animal that flies over the earth carrying on its back three precious jewels, bringing these invaluable gifts to all humanity: the Buddha (the 'awakened one') his teaching, and the community of all his followers.

Windhorse Publications
169 Mill Road
Cambridge CB1 3AN
UK
info@windhorsepublications.com

Perseus Distribution
1094 Flex Drive
Jackson TN 38301
USA

Windhorse Books
PO Box 574
Newtown NSW 2042
Australia

THE TRIRATNA BUDDHIST COMMUNITY

Windhorse Publications is a part of the Triratna Buddhist Community, which has more than sixty centres on five continents. Through these centres, members of the Triratna Buddhist Order offer classes in meditation and Buddhism, from an introductory to deeper levels of commitment. Bodywork classes such as yoga, Tai chi, and massage are also taught at many Triratna centres. Members of the Triratna community run retreat centres around the world, and the Karuna Trust, a UK fundraising charity that supports social welfare projects in the slums and villages of South Asia.

Many Triratna centres have residential spiritual communities and ethical Right Livelihood businesses associated with them. Arts activities are encouraged too, as is the development of strong bonds of friendship between people who share the same ideals. In this way Triratna is developing a unique approach to Buddhism, not simply as a set of techniques, but as a creatively directed way of life for people living in the modern world.

If you would like more information about Triratna please visit www.thebuddhistcentre.com or write to:

London Buddhist Centre
51 Roman Road
London E2 0HU
UK

Aryaloka
14 Heartwood Circle
Newmarket NH 03857
USA

Sydney Buddhist Centre
24 Enmore Road
Sydney NSW 2042
Australia

Also from Windhorse Publications

A Buddhist View series

Solitude and Loneliness: A Buddhist View
by Sarvananda

Charlie Chaplin observed, 'Loneliness is the theme of everyone.'
Although true, it is equally true that we all very skillfully, and often
unconsciously, organize our lives in such a way as to avoid loneliness.

Drawing on a wide range of sources – the poets Dickinson and Hafiz,
the painter Edward Hopper, the sage Milarepa, the lives of Helen
Keller and Chris McCandless, and of course the Buddha – Sarvananda
explores the themes of isolation, loneliness and solitude from a
Buddhist perspective and examines how and why our relationship to
ourselves can be a source of both suffering and liberation.

ISBN 9781 907314 07 0
£8.99 / $13.95 / €10.95
152 pages

Finding the Mind: A Buddhist View
by Robin Cooper

'Here am I, in this body I call my own, among millions that are mysteriously other. What's going on?' You may have asked this, or something like it, at some point in your life. How can you find the answer?

Buddhism points to your own mind as a way to understand and transform your experience. But, as Robin Cooper explains, it takes an exploratory approach, it asks you to seek: it is not a revelation of religious truths. The Buddha saw that we are all in a tough predicament. We are constantly anxious about what we lack and what we may lose, and in chasing security we easily cause pain to others. But the Buddha did not offer to save us through faith in his truth. Instead, he asked us to explore. Be aware, probe the edges of your awareness, investigate, and find your mind.

ISBN 9781 9073140 3 2
£8.99 / $13.95 / € 10.95
160 pages

Buddhism: Tools for Living Your Life
by Vajragupta

In this guide for all those seeking a meaningful spiritual path, Vajragupta provides clear explanations of the main Buddhist teachings, as well as a variety of exercises designed to help readers develop or deepen their practice.

Appealing, readable, and practical, blending accessible teachings, practices, and personal stories . . . as directly relevant to modern life as it is comprehensive and rigorous. – Tricycle: The Buddhist Review, 2007

I'm very pleased that someone has finally written this book! At last, a real 'toolkit' for living a Buddhist life, his practical suggestions are hard to resist! – Saddhanandi, Chair of Taraloka Retreat Centre

ISBN 9781 899579 74 7
£10.99 / $16.95 / €16.95
192 pages

The Triratna Story: Behind the Scenes of a New Buddhist Movement
by Vajragupta

This is the story of a circle of friends dreaming a dream, and working to make it a reality. It's the nitty-gritty tale of how a community evolves. It's a record of idealism and naivety, growth and growing pains, hard work and burn-out, friendship and fall-out. It's a celebration of how so much was achieved in so short a time, and a reflection on the mistakes made, and lessons learnt.

An excellent synopsis of the history of an important Buddhist movement. – David Brazier, author and head of the Amida-Shu.

. . .a courageous and important book. – Zoketsu Norman Fischer, author and founder of the Everyday Zen Foundation.

ISBN 9781 899579 92 1
£7.99 / $13.95 / €8.95
224 pages

A Guide to the Buddhist Path
by Sangharakshita

The Buddhist tradition, with its numerous schools and teachings, can understandably feel daunting. Which teachings really matter? How can one begin to practice Buddhism in a systematic way? This can be confusing territory. Without a guide one can easily get dispirited or lost.

Profoundly experienced in Buddhist practice, intimately familiar with its main schools, and founder of the Triratna Buddhist Community, Sangharakshita is the ideal guide. In this highly readable anthology he sorts out fact from myth and theory from practice to reveal the principle ideals and teachings of Buddhism. The result is a reliable and far-reaching guide to this inspiring path.

ISBN 9781 907314 05 6
£16.99 / $23.95 / €19.95
264 pages

The Buddha's Noble Eightfold Path
by Sangharakshita

The Noble Eightfold Path is the most widely known of the Buddha's teachings. It is ancient, extending back to the Buddha's first discourse and is highly valued as a unique treasury of wisdom and practical guidance on how to live our lives.

This introduction takes the reader deeper while always remaining practical, inspiring and accessible. Sangharakshita translates ancient teachings and makes them relevant to the way we live our lives today.

Probably the best 'life coaching' manual you'll ever read, the key to living with clarity and awareness. – Karen Robinson, *The Sunday Times*

ISBN 9781 899579 81 5
£9.99 / $16.95 / €16.95
176 pages

Visions of Mahayana Buddhism
by Nagapriya

In a unique overview of this inspiring tradition, Nagapriya introduces its themes and huge spectrum of practices, literature, and movements. Charting the evolution and expression of the Mahayana as a whole, he tracks its movement across South and East Asia, uncovering its history, culture, and doctrines and blending this extensive knowledge with a strong element of lived practice.

Ideal for both teaching and personal use, this far-reaching and imaginative guide provides a solid foundation for any study in Buddhism and a valuable voice on Asian history.

A very helpful introduction and overview of this complex, fascinating tradition. – David R. Loy, author of *Money, Sex, War, Karma*

ISBN 9781 899579 97 6
£12.99 / $21.95 / €16.95
288 pages

A Path for Parents
by Sara Burns

A Path for Parents is for anyone interested in spiritual life within the context of parenting. Sara Burns, mother and Buddhist practitioner, draws on her own experience to deliver a refreshingly honest and accessible account of how parents can grow spiritually among their everyday experiences of life with children.

ISBN 9781 899579 70 9
£11.99 / $17.95 / €17.95
176 pages

The Three Jewels series
by Sangharakshita

This set of three essential texts introduces the Three Jewels which are central to Buddhism: the *Buddha* (the Enlightened One), the *Dharma* (the Buddha's teachings), and the *Sangha* (the spiritual community).

Who is the Buddha?

ISBN 9781 899579 51 8
£8.99 / $14.95 / €11.95
188 pages

What is the Dharma?

ISBN 9781 899579 01 3
£9.99 / $19.95 / €12.95
272 pages

What is the Sangha?

ISBN 9781 899579 31 0
£9.99 / $19.95 / €12.95
288 pages

Meeting the Buddhas series

by Vessantara

This set of three informative guides, by one of our best-selling authors, introduces the historical and archetypal figures from within the Tibetan Buddhist tradition. Each book focuses on a different set of figures and features full-colour illustrations.

A Guide to the Buddhas

ISBN 9781 899579 83 9
£11.99 / $18.95 / €18.95
176 pages

A Guide to the Bodhisattvas

ISBN 9781 899579 84 6
£11.99 / $18.95 / €18.95
128 pages

A Guide to the Deities of the Tantra

ISBN 9781 899579 85 3
£11.99 / $18.95 / €18.95
192 pages

Buddhist Wisdom in Practice series

The Art of Reflection
by Ratnaguna

It is all too easy either to think obsessively, or to not think enough. But how do we think usefully? How do we reflect? Like any art, reflection can be learnt and developed, leading to a deeper understanding of life and to the fullness of wisdom. *The Art of Reflection* is a practical guide to reflection as a spiritual practice, about "what we think and how we think about it". It is a book about contemplation and insight, and reflection as a way to discover the truth.

No-one who takes seriously the study and practice of the Dharma should fail to read this ground-breaking book. – Sangharakshita, founder of the Triratna Buddhist Community

ISBN 9781 899579 89 1
£9.99 / $16.95 / €11.95
160 pages

This Being, That Becomes
by Dhivan Thomas Jones

Dhivan Thomas Jones takes us into the heart of the Buddha's insight that everything arises in dependence on conditions. With the aid of lucid reflections and exercises he prompts us to explore how conditionality works in our own lives, and provides a sure guide to the most essential teaching of Buddhism.

Clearly and intelligently written, this book carries a lot of good advice. Prof Richard Gombrich, author of *What the Buddha Thought*.

ISBN 9781 899579 90 7
£12.99 / $20.95 / €15.95
216 pages